YOU WIN IN THE LOCKER ROOM FIRST

YOU WIN IN THE LOCKER ROOM FIRST

7 C's to Build a Winning Team in
Sports, Business, and Life

JON GORDON

MIKE SMITH

WILEY

To Julie, for always being there for me.
To Logan, for all of your patience while I worked on this project with Jon.
To my mom and dad, for all of your love and guidance.
To all the coaches, players, and support staff that I have worked with and coached against. Thank you for helping me have a better understanding of the greatest sport of all.

—Mike Smith

To Kathryn, thank you for being my lifelong teammate.
To Jade and Cole, for helping me be a better coach and parent.
To my mom and dad, for believing in me.
To all the leaders, coaches, and teams who have shared your experiences and wisdom with me. This book would not have been possible without you.

—Jon Gordon

Contents

Introduction

By Mike Smith

I've been a coach for 32 years and half of that time was in the NFL. I was on the staff of the Baltimore Ravens when we won the Super Bowl, and I was one play away from going to the Super Bowl as head coach of the Atlanta Falcons. For five years we had the second most wins in the NFL—only Bill Belichick and the Patriots had more. I'm also a coach that was fired because during my last two seasons with the Falcons we only had 10 wins combined. Looking back, I can see clearly the difference between those first five seasons and the last two. I understand why we won and why we lost. In this book, Jon and I aim to help you build a winning team and avoid the mistakes made by too many leaders, including me. Jon and I often talk about the fact that success happens by focusing on the process, not the outcome. You win by cultivating the right culture, leadership, expectations, beliefs, mindset, relationships, and habits before you even play the game. You win in the locker room first. Then, you win on the field.

I've known Jon for over 10 years. We first met when I was the defensive coordinator with the Jacksonville Jaguars and our head athletic trainer Mike Ryan introduced us. Our team read his book *The Energy Bus,* and Jon spoke to our team during training camp. We had an incredible season, went to the playoffs, and beat the Steelers in Pittsburgh in the first round.

When I became the head coach for the Atlanta Falcons the next year, I knew I wanted to bring *The Energy Bus* and Jon to our team as well. I had all the guys read the book and Jon spoke to our team. We focused on implementing many of the principles in this book. We went from a losing record of 4 and 12 to 11 and 5 and we made it to the playoffs. I'll tell you more about that turnaround in a little bit, but for now it's important for you to know that Jon and I have spent eight training camps together and each year we have talked about using the seven C's to build a great team and win in the locker room first. I have my favorite C's and Jon has his.

Since Jon and I first began working together, he has also helped countless teams in the NFL, MLB, NBA, and NCAA. He has had the luxury of seeing what other coaches do to build their teams and has amassed a ton of knowledge and best practices. He became very passionate about his C's and I grew confident about my own favorites since I had seen the impact firsthand. Jon and I would often debate about which were most important.

After my last year with the Falcons and seeing what happened to our culture the last two seasons compared to the first five seasons, we know without a doubt that winning in the locker room begins foremost with culture. So let's start there. Jon and I will share what we know about building winning teams and we truly hope it helps you develop and grow your team.

Chapter 1

Culture

Culture drives expectations and beliefs;
expectations and beliefs drive behavior;
behavior drives habits;
and habits create the future.
It all starts with culture.

Create a Winning Culture

Mike Smith

 In January of 2008 I was hired as the head coach of the Atlanta Falcons. Most of the time when head coaches are hired, they are not coming into a very good or stable situation. It is not the norm to replace a coach who has just won the Super Bowl and is riding off into the sunset, like Bill Walsh after Super Bowl XXXIII or Bill Cowher who only coached one more season after Super Bowl XL. When I was named the coach of the Atlanta Falcons, they were a team that had been through quite a bit of recent turmoil and struggled to win consistently throughout the history of the franchise. In their 42 years, the Atlanta Falcons had never had back-to-back winning seasons. They had always for some reason or another struggled with consistency and sustainability. For example, from 2000 to 2007 the Falcons had five different men stand on the sideline in the role of head coach. The 2007 season had been an extremely difficult one, in which the first-year head coach had resigned after 12 games— three-quarters through the season—to return to coach at the college level. The quarterback, who was not only the face of the franchise but also without a doubt one of the most popular players in the NFL, was headed to federal prison. While none of this was the fault of the ownership and executives of the Falcons organization, such extreme and unfortunate events can create a challenging, almost dysfunctional, working environment. Needless to say, the culture of the team was in shambles.

Jon and I talked several times on the phone about the state of the Falcons' organization and it became very clear that if I was going to turn this team around, the first step would be to focus on transforming the culture. While the football coach in me wanted to attack the X and O issues and work with first-year general manger Thomas Dimitroff to calibrate the roster for the upcoming season, I knew the biggest priority was to create a winning culture in which every member could thrive and excel. This meant we would not only have to create the right culture for the team but also for the rest of the organization.

Build Your Culture Up and Down

Mike Smith

I've always believed that culture is defined and created from the top down, but it comes to life from the bottom up. This meant that I had to build our culture by working with the leadership group (i.e., the owner, general manager, and executives), the coaching staff, and the football team. To strengthen the culture among the leadership group, it was important to reiterate to the owner, team president, and general manager the shared beliefs, values, and expectations that we had discussed in depth when I was interviewing for the head coaching position. It was important to have collaborative conversations on a regular basis to discuss the changes we were making and why we were making them.

To develop a strong culture on the team level, we started to evaluate players on their character and attitudes in addition to their football skills. Changes to the roster were not solely based on the players' abilities on the field. We also looked very closely at the intangibles that each player would bring to the locker room. We wanted to have team members who were going to positively represent the organization on and off the field. It was important that we had players who were going to be good teammates and citizens.

We made sure that our owner, Arthur Blank, knew why we were making these adjustments to the roster and how they supported the culture we were trying to create. We had to make it clear that these changes, both by addition and subtraction, were going to be about upgrading our roster both on and off the field. All of these moves were in line with the coaching philosophy, values, and principles that we had talked about before I signed on as head coach. We were not going to be adding any outliers to our organization, no matter how much talent they had. With support from the owner and the organization's top leadership, Thomas and I set out to build a new team culture from the ground up.

During the first off-season, Thomas and I worked very closely. It was not unusual to have multiple daily meetings. We made a very conscious effort to make sure that we met at the start and the end of every day to discuss all facets of football operations. Meetings about personnel always involved what a

5

Culture

player could bring to the locker room and the culture of the team. We both knew that building a team would be much more complex than just adding the best available athletes. We also had discussions about how the support staff and the interaction between football operations and the rest of the organization were progressing.

It wasn't enough to just build a team culture. To have sustained success, we needed a winning organizational culture, and I knew that by working closely with the leadership group to define and set the culture, we would be able to have that. I needed the owner and leaders to buy in and be an integral part of the process. Their buy-in needed to be as deep as the players'. I also knew that to create a successful team on the field, I needed to involve more than just leadership, players, and staff. We needed *everyone* in the organization to buy in.

Everyone Creates Your Culture

Mike Smith

Culture consists of the shared purpose, attitudes, values, goals, practices, behaviors, and habits that define a team or organization. Many coaches focus only on the culture shared by the players, but the fact is that everyone in an organization shapes the culture. To be successful, you need everyone in your organization thinking, believing, talking, and behaving in sync. You need everyone to be aligned with the same beliefs, expectations, behaviors, and habits. Thomas and I learned quickly that the beliefs and behaviors of the past had to go and we needed to instill new ways of thinking and acting that everyone could follow.

For this reason, when I gave the team Jon Gordon's book *The Energy Bus* that first year, I also gave it to everyone else in the organization. I wanted us all thinking the same way. *Everyone* included the executive team, operations people, sales and marketing folks, equipment managers, maintenance staff, food service workers, and anyone else in the building. Reaching everyone in the Atlanta Falcons organization was a challenge, but I made it a priority to connect with everyone in the organization, and distributing Jon's book was a part of this process.

Besides getting *The Energy Bus* into the hands of as many people in the organization as possible, I spent the majority of my time those first few months as head coach meeting with as many people as possible, to introduce myself and have conversations about their specific jobs. It was important for them to know that their roles in the organization were important and that they were going to be an integral part of our team's success in the future. I didn't want there to be one culture in the locker room and a different culture in the rest of the building. I wanted us to be *one team*, with *one culture*. I believed that because the support staff and members of the off-field departments came into contact with our players, they should also share a positive attitude. Their outlook and pride in their work would enhance our chances of being an organization that can be great both on and off the field. While it was obvious that the players needed to help build a winning team, it was just as important for the people outside the locker room to enjoy being part of the process. I let everyone know that my role was to assist them in doing their jobs and together we would build a winning team. Then, throughout the years, I backed up my words with actions, and I believe this had a big impact on our overall culture and success. As a leader, it is so important that your words equal your actions. It is imperative that you make sure that you go through a self-evaluation process on an almost daily basis to make sure that your actions are in line with your words. You must do what you say and say what you do.

X's and O's Are Overrated

Mike Smith

Professional athletics is probably the most competitive industry in the world. The NFL is designed for parity in many ways, with a hard salary cap, free agency, and the draft system. During my seven years in Atlanta, 22 percent of all games played in the NFL were decided by three or fewer points and 45 percent of the games were decided by seven or fewer points. When almost half the games come down to the final possession, it makes the margin for error very small. I guess that is why the game is so popular and the phrase "on any given Sunday" is so true.

With the competition so heated, everyone is looking for an edge. Teams spend millions of dollars every year trying to gain an advantage and be better than the rest of the league. They will spend money on athletic performance, analytics, coordinators who offer new offensive and defensive schemes, and so on. All of those have merit and you have to be doing everything possible to improve your organization. When you are dealing with the best athletes and coaches in the world, there is a fine line between winning and losing. You have to be well prepared both physically and mentally to go out and compete each week. You must have a great game plan, and it's essential for coaches to call the right plays and for players to execute effectively. Strategy is important. Execution is imperative. However, the most overlooked aspect in team sports, and what most coaches and leaders fail to grasp, is the fact that it is your culture that will determine whether your strategy works and is sustainable. It is the culture you create that is going to determine whether your players perform and execute.

Every week you will face very difficult circumstances that are completely out of your control. There are going to be injuries that effect match-ups, the ball is not going to bounce your way, and there will be mistakes made both by players and coaches. The strategies and game plans are going to change from week to week. In the face of all this, it is your culture that will be the driving force to create the resiliency, toughness, passion, and attitude to overcome the obstacles in your way. The wildcat came and went. The spread option was hot for a year or two. Certain plays work for a while until opposing teams figure them out. X's and O's are important but culture is the rock that your organization must be built upon—and if you do it the right way, you'll have sustained success, as we did for five years. The last two years are another story, however, and later on I'm going to share what we learned from that.

Sustained Culture = Sustained Success

Jon Gordon

I couldn't agree more with Mike about the importance of culture. Mike and I had many conversations about culture and it was very exciting to see him put his beliefs and plan into action. As someone who writes, speaks, and thinks a lot about culture, I loved watching the principles take hold in real life. Theory is one thing; practical application is another. But what Mike did and the way he did it is a great demonstration of why organizations with sustained cultures have sustained success. Culture drives expectations and beliefs. Expectations and beliefs drive behaviors. Behaviors drive habits and habits create the future. If you look at the most successful organizations in business, sports, health care, and education you notice they all have great cultures. Indeed X's and O's are overrated. I once spoke at a football clinic years ago on the topic of culture. I had five people in my session. The workshop on X's and O's had 500 people in it. I knew then that most people don't understand that X's and O's won't sustain success. Culture will. You must spend more time on building your culture than on everything else. Culture is what produces wins over time.

Know What You Stand For

Jon Gordon

If you are looking to build a new culture or transform the one you have, the first questions you should ask yourself are, "What do we stand for?" and "What do we want to be known for?" For example, for my book *The Hard Hat*, I interviewed coach Jeff Tambroni, who helped build Cornell lacrosse into a national powerhouse, to ask him how he did it. He said, "We know who our people are. We know who fits our culture." Jeff built a culture that was defined by a blue-collar work ethic (symbolized by a hard hat), as well as selflessness, teamwork, relentless effort, and continuous improvement. By knowing what their culture stood for, Jeff and his staff were able to choose the right people who fit their culture. When you know what you stand for you can find the right people who stand for the same things as you. Brad Stevens, the head coach of the Boston Celtics, told me that your culture is not just your tradition. It is the people in the locker room who carry it on. When you have people who fit your culture and carry it on, it comes to life in a powerful way.

Knowing what you stand for is just as important in the business world. When Apple was just the two Steves (Steve Jobs and Steve Wozniak), they knew the culture they wanted to create. They wanted to challenge the status quo. Everything they did was influenced by their culture: the people they hired, the products they created, and the campaigns they ran. This approach still influences everything at Apple. Apple is famous for saying that culture beats strategy. What you stand for drives everything else.

I had the opportunity to speak to Southwest Airlines a few years ago, and they told me how consultants suggested they charge passengers to check luggage since the competition was doing it and they could make millions of dollars in additional revenue. Southwest considered their proposal but in the process asked themselves an important question: "Is this what we stand for?" They went straight to their purpose statement: "To connect people to what's important in their lives through friendly, reliable, and low-cost air travel." They ultimately decided that if they were for everyday fliers and low-cost air travel, they shouldn't charge baggage fees. You would think they would have missed out on a lot of money, but a funny thing happened. Southwest started to get new customers because the airline didn't charge for bags. They ran advertising campaigns highlighting the fact that bags fly free, and they gained market share in the process. Their revenue grew to new heights. It's a great example that once you know what you stand for, decisions are easy to make. Both your strategic decisions and those made on the fly. When your culture dictates your decisions you will enjoy sustained success.

Process and Milestones

Mike Smith

Knowing what you stand for is essential. From the moment I took over as the coach of the Atlanta Falcons, I knew the kind of culture we needed to create and I defined it for the team. The seven responsibilities everyone had were to:

1. Have fun, work hard, and enjoy the journey.

2. Show respect for every person you have contact with in the organization.

3. Put the team first. Successful teams have teammates that are unselfish and willing to put their individual goals behind the team's goals.

4. Do your job. It is defined, but you must always be prepared for it to change (especially if you're a player).

5. Appropriately handle victory and defeat, adulation and humiliation. Do not get too high in victory or too low in defeat. Be the same person every day.

6. Understand that all organizational decisions aim to make the team better, stronger, and more efficient.

7. Have a positive attitude. Use positive language (both verbal and body language).

I told our team each year that if we were able to consistently meet these expectations, then we would be well on our way to establishing a culture where team members can thrive in the ultimately competitive NFL. I also made it very clear from the beginning that we were going to be a team that focused on the process of preparing for each practice and game, not on the outcome of our entire season.

Don't get me wrong; the NFL is all about results, and teams are ultimately judged by the number of wins and losses that they accumulate each year. If you don't win enough, you will get fired. I even joked with our general manager, Thomas, when I took the job that he didn't hire me to retire me; he hired me to fire me. It was just going to be a matter of time. Very rarely does the coach get to leave on his own terms in today's NFL. Thomas and I had many discussions about how we wanted to beat the odds so I could be one of the few that go out on their own terms. Those first five years, we were well on our way to accomplishing that goal. Prior to the start of the 2014 season, there were only six coaches in the league that had longer tenures at the same team than my six seasons in Atlanta. Amazingly, during my seven years as head coach, the league saw 66 head-coaching changes. That is the equivalent of the entire league turning over more than twice. You can see why former Falcons coach Jerry Glanville in 1988 said that, when it comes to head coaches, NFL stands for "Not for Long."

So when it came to outcomes, you bet I wanted to win. I wanted to coach as long as possible and win as much as we could, but I knew the best way to do this was to *not* focus on a season's outcome, but instead use a practice-to-practice, game-to-game process. My intention from the beginning was not to focus on goals, but on preparation and milestones. After all, every team in the league has the same goals so it's not your goals that will lead to your success but your commitment to the process, one game at a time, that will define your season.

When we had our first team meeting of the off-season, the message was that we were going to focus on the process of building the team. The majority of the first meeting was to explain the sequencing of an NFL season. The team was shown the layout of every practice up to the start of the first week of the season, and the entire off-season program was laid out for them in detail. When I say detail I mean *detail*. The coaching staff had accounted for every minute in the meeting rooms and on the practice field. It was important for players to see that the entire off-season had to be planned and that everyone knew what we would be doing every single day in the classroom, in the weight room, and on the field. The players were aware that we were going to be very systematic in the way that we prepared. They knew the exact number of plays that we were going to run in the off-season and the amount of time that was going to be invested into the different situations that could arise in a game. There were not going to be any surprises in terms of what we did in our meetings and on the field. We were not going to concern ourselves with our overall record; instead, we were going to focus on mastering the skills to be the absolute best team we could be in 2008.

As we got to the opening week of the season, I addressed the team about how we had progressed through the off-season programs, mini-camps, and the preseason. We felt that we had made great strides in the progression of preparing for the grind of the NFL season. It was at the Monday meeting prior to the start of the season that I told our team that we were not going to have any goals in the traditional sense, and that we all knew how we were going to be evaluated at the end of the season. I told them that we were going to focus on *milestones* and that after we accomplished one, we would be presented with the next. The first milestone was to win a game and we were going to get that chance the coming Sunday. They were also told the importance of first impressions. You only get one chance at a first impression and that moment, good or bad, usually sets the tone for the season. We definitely took advantage of leaving a great first impression. The very first pass attempt of the season was a 62-yard touchdown throw from Matt Ryan to Michael Jenkins. After that, we went on to win the game. First milestone accomplished. The next milestone was to start a streak and win on the road. Despite the positive energy that remained after our first-game win, we lost the next game, and our milestone shifted. Now instead of starting a winning streak, we aimed to avoid back-to-back losses. I let the team know that if we could go the entire season without losing back-to-back games and put together at least one two-game winning streak, we were going to like where we were in November. After that, we made it a milestone to beat our division opponents because winning our division would be the most direct path to the playoffs (or as some call it, the *second season*). After each new game, I presented a new milestone to attempt to accomplish. I told them that the more milestones we were able to reach, the better our standing would be at the end of the season. In 2008, our focus was on the journey, not the destination. We looked up in December and clinched a playoff berth in our first season.

Focus on the Root, Not the Fruit

Mike Smith

Milestones and process were a big part of our culture and philosophy those first five years and, as a result, we had unprecedented success as a team and organization. But sometimes success can be your worst enemy if you allow it to change your culture and approach. Jon had often told me that if you focus on the fruit and ignore the root, the tree will die, but if you continue to care for the root and focus on your culture, process, people, and purpose, then you'll always have a great supply of fruit. Those first five years, we focused a lot on the root and had a lot of fruit. We won a lot. Our culture was strong. But then we fell one play short of going to the Super Bowl. In the 2012 NFC Championship game, we were 10 yards away from winning the game. We had put together a six-minute drive and had the ball on the San Francisco 49ers' 10-yard line. It was third and four with just over a minute to play. Matt Ryan was knocked to the ground on an incomplete pass and injured his shoulder, but, as he had done so many times in his first five years, he showed his resilience and continued playing. No one realized how serious his injury was, and on fourth down, Matt's pass attempt to Roddy White was incomplete. With that, our chances of playing in the Super Bowl against the Baltimore Ravens—where I had previously coached—evaporated.

After that, everything changed. As an organization, we felt we had been one play away from going to the Super Bowl and, suddenly, getting there became the only thing we cared about. As an organization, we were obsessed. Unfortunately, that affected the way the team and the organization approached the upcoming season. Instead of starting over from the beginning and continuing to focus on the process, one practice and one game at a time, we only cared about the outcome. We stopped setting milestones and only focused on getting back to the playoffs. If we didn't make it to the Super Bowl, the season would be considered a failure by the media, our fan base, and many within our organization. The pressure was on, and all of us felt it—our ownership, our quarterback, our team, and me—and, looking back, I allowed the pressure to steer us away from the very things that made us successful. I didn't fight enough for our culture. I stopped building the culture up and down. I did a very poor job of making sure the new members of the team, staff, and organization understood the culture that we had worked so hard to create. We all learned the hard way that culture can change almost as quickly as the momentum in a football game. Looking back, it's not a surprise that in our last two seasons we experienced the outcomes we did. I let outside forces and pressure weaken our culture. When we stopped tending to the root, the sports world saw our tree wither.

You Have to Fight for Your Culture and Team

Mike Smith

Nothing better demonstrates how much our culture had withered than the second half of the 2014 season. As we were fighting for a playoff spot despite having a losing record, the signs were obvious that the culture within our organization was not healthy. As an organization you want to do everything in your power to minimize and eliminate distractions for the players and coaches so your team can focus on being their best on the field. The last thing you want is for your own organization to be the cause of the distraction. Unfortunately that's exactly what happened as we were trying to make the playoffs.

The self-inflicted distractions started prior to the Monday night game played in Green Bay. An article was written in the *New York Post* and was attributed to an unnamed source within our organization. The article stated that the coach of the Jets would be the choice of the owner if the Falcons made a change. Unfortunately we lost the game against Green Bay and it only made people wonder if the report was true. I didn't think much about the report at the time but it did hit me that in my six-and-a-half years with the Falcons we never had a report with an unnamed source and all of a sudden, there was one.

In week 16 against the New Orleans Saints, the morning of the game it was reported that if the Falcons lost to the Saints that I was going to be fired according to a source with the team. Not something that you want your team to see scrolling across the bottom of the TV screen at the pregame meal and in the locker room. Thankfully we went out and played one of our best games of the year and won. It set up the "winner goes to the playoff" game against the Carolina Panthers the next week. I was happy that we won but again it struck me as strange that there was another unnamed source discussing my coaching future.

The morning of the "winner goes to the playoff" game against Carolina, at the pre-game meal, it happened again. In the pregame shows it is reported that the Falcons have hired a search firm to assist in the search for a head coach if the Falcons make a change. Are you kidding me? We have a chance to make the playoffs and someone within the organization is leaking this news to the press. Unfortunately we went out and played probably the worst game in our seven year tenure. Even worse, I let it happen.

Through the first six seasons I showed the players on the team that I would literally fight for them. Whether it was telling a trash talking player from an opposing team to shut his mouth and get off our sideline or getting in the middle of a scrum on our sideline and getting fined by the league office for making physical contact with an opposing player, my team knew that I was all in with them and was willing to fight for them both mentally and physically. But when the unnamed sources and news leaks started happening, I didn't fight for the team like I should have. I thought that if we won, the leaks and news would go away. I was focused on the outcome instead of fighting for my team and culture. People often ask me who was leaking the information, but truthfully I really don't care. That is not the issue here. What matters most is that I did not ever formally address these three specific incidents internally and externally. I did not fight for my team. I needed to attack this straight on. Each media report was a major distraction and did not give our team the best chance to go through our preparation, focus, and win. I should have addressed the news reports with the team. I should have called an urgent meeting with our leadership team, addressed the news leaks, and demanded that whoever was doing it needed to stop sabotaging his own team. Instead of hoping that winning would solve the situation, I should have not let this situation happen. I helped create our culture and I should have fought for it until the end. I have made many mistakes along the way. No leader is perfect. But this was one mistake I wish I could do over.

I'm sorry it happened, but now it's one of the most valuable lessons I've ever learned, and one that I can share with you so you don't make the same mistake. That's why I want to encourage you to build your culture, value it, live it, reinforce it, and fight for it. Make sure the new people joining the team and organization know what you stand for. No matter what happens, whether you win or lose, keep focusing on the root. Forget what happened last season. You must have amnesia about past negative outcomes and a great memory of all the little things you did to create success. Focus on the process and don't let outside or inside forces sabotage your culture. My first five years are an indication of what happens when you stay true to your culture and process, and my last two years are a great example of what happens when you don't.

So now that you know what went wrong those last two years, let's talk about what we did right the first five years and how we built our culture and team with the additional C's, starting with *contagious* energy. If you focus on what Jon and I share with you and stay true to your culture, I'm confident you'll experience sustained success.

Chapter 2

Contagious

Leadership is a transfer of purpose,
passion, optimism, and belief.

Germer or Vitamin C?

Jon Gordon

 Research from the HeartMath Institute (heartmath.org) shows that when you have a feeling in your heart, it goes to every cell in the body, then outward—and other people up to 10 feet away can sense feelings transmitted by your heart. This means that each day you are broadcasting to your team how you feel. You are either broadcasting positive energy or negative energy, apathy or passion, indifference or purpose. Research from Harvard University also supports that idea that the emotions you feel are contagious and affect the people around you. Your team is just as likely to catch your bad mood as the swine flu, and on the flip side, they will catch your good mood as well. And this principle applies to everyone, not just the leader. Each member of your team is contagious and every day you all are either sharing positive or negative energy with each other. Great cultures are built with positive contagious energy so it's essential that you and your team share it. When you walk into the locker room, the office, or onto the field, you have a decision to make: Are you going to be a germ to your team or a big dose of vitamin C? Will you infuse your team

with positive energy or be an energy vampire and suck the life out of them?

Great leaders and teams are positively contagious with a vision and purpose that drives them, positive thoughts that fuel them, and emotions that energize them. Great leaders and teammates realize that their overall attitudes affect everyone in the locker room and the building.

Contagious with a Vision and Mission

Jon Gordon

A powerful way for leaders to be contagious is to share a positive vision and mission with their team. Every team needs a vision and mission to unite them and serve as a North Star to guide them in the right direction. Your vision and mission should be simple, clear, bold, and compelling. I'm not talking about a string of buzzwords and jargon that mean nothing to your team members, but rather something tangible and exciting to serve as a rallying cry and focal point for your team. Taking an example from the business world, long before "Let's Build a Smarter Planet" was IBM's advertising tagline, the phrase served as an internal vision and mission for everyone to sell, build, and design projects that made data more useful for clients.

Doug Conant, the former CEO of the Campbell Soup Company, told me that the most important thing he did when leading Campbell's turnaround was to share the vision and mission statement with everyone in the company. He said he did so at every meeting and as often as he could in order to keep everyone moving in the right direction. Their vision and mission was "Together we will build the world's most extraordinary food company by nourishing people's lives everywhere, every day." General Motors rejuvenated their mission, brand, and sales with a simple focused vision and mission, "To design, build and sell the world's best vehicles." USAA keeps everyone in their organization focused on their mission and vision that they are here to "Facilitate the financial security of its members, associates and their families by providing a full range of highly competitive financial products and services. In doing so, we hope to be the provider of choice for the military community."

When speaking to leaders of sports teams I encourage them to create a mission statement that doesn't mention winning a championship. After all, every football team has a goal to win the Super Bowl at the beginning of an NFL season, but merely stating that goal won't help you achieve it. Your success comes from your team's commitment to a vision and purpose. I believe that a vision and mission should include the greatness you want to chase with a focus on the character traits and purpose that inspire you to get there.

Some teams I have worked with made it their mission to be the toughest, hardest working team in the league. Other teams decided they were playing for their community and families. Some play to honor their tradition and leave a legacy. In *The Hard Hat*, I share how the Cornell Lacrosse team played to honor their teammate who had died playing the game they loved.

Research shows that people are most energized when they are contributing to a bigger cause beyond themselves. As a leader, you want to inspire your team to move beyond their own selfish desires and concerns and contribute to a cause bigger than them. When your team has a greater vision and purpose they will play with greater passion and energy. I can't tell you what your vision and mission should be but I can tell you they are essential to unite and rally your team. You can create this vision, mission, and purpose as a leadership group and share it with your team. When possible, create it with your team members.

Contagious with Your Belief

Jon Gordon

Winning doesn't begin just in the locker room; it also begins in the mind. You win in the mind first and then you win on the field or court. Often the difference between success and failure is belief. Does a team believe they can win? Have their preparation, practice, and focus given them the confidence that they can? Do they stay positive and optimistic through adversity and challenges? Pete Carroll said, "The world trains people to be pessimistic . . . one of the most important things I must do here is to make sure my players and staff believe that tomorrow will be better than today." Leadership is a transfer of belief and it's essential that you share positive beliefs with your team, especially from the beginning. The minute the season starts, it's time to set the tone and cultivate the right belief system. You can't wait until adversity happens to do this. Start from the beginning, and you will be strong when challenges come your way. I'm convinced one of the most important things a leader must do is to be positive and optimistic. The research supports this and actually shows that optimism is a competitive advantage. Manju Puri and David Robinson at Duke University found that optimistic people work harder, get paid more, win at sports more regularly, get elected to office more often, and live longer! It turns out that being positive is not just a nice, feel-good way to live but is, in fact, *the* way to live if you want better health, more meaningful relationships, and greater individual and team success.

I've witnessed the power of belief firsthand working with Clemson football and Dabo Swinney. When asked how Clemson has achieved at least 10 wins in each of the past four seasons for the first time in school history, Dabo said, "People often call me an overachiever, but I'm not an overachiever. I'm an over-believer." Dabo believes in his team so much that he inspires them to believe in themselves. Every meeting with his team is an opportunity for him to tell them what they can achieve if they truly believe. At every practice, he raises their expectations and then inspires them to rise up and meet these expectations. Like Apple founder Steve Jobs, he inspires them to believe they can do more, create more, and become more than they ever thought possible. Steve Jobs was famous for what Apple employees called his *reality distortion field*. In Walter Isaacson's biography *Steve Jobs*, he describes how Steve could convince the Apple team that they could meet a project deadline that everyone thought was impossible. Time and time again, they would actually do it. Steve's team said he distorted their reality from pessimism (or some would say realism) to optimism. His belief was contagious and Apple became one of the greatest companies on Earth as a result. What could your team achieve if you were contagious with optimism and belief?

Contagious with a Positive Attitude

Mike Smith

Like most things, when it comes to belief, if you don't have it you can't share it. As a coach, I always knew I had to share positive beliefs with my team and this meant I had to fill my mind with the right thoughts and maintain a positive attitude. Shortly after I was hired in Atlanta I wrote down the expectations I had for myself. The first one that I wrote in my notes was "Never a bad day, only bad moments." This was a commitment to never let myself have a bad day. It did not matter how many bad or challenging moments would occur; at the end of the day, I would make sure to identify enough good and uplifting moments to declare it a good day. It is so much easier to deal with and overcome the bad moments when you think about how fortunate you are to have an opportunity to impact and lead others. So instead of allowing myself to focus on the negative, I created moments of gratitude and focused on the positive. Sure there were days when I had to really work to find the good, but I still found it and did my best to share a positive attitude with everyone in the building.

Head coaches work not only with players and other coaches, but they also have to interact with a number of different people throughout the building. Depending on the day and time of year, I met with coaches, players, the owner, our team president, the general manager, trainers, team doctors, travel and logistics people, members of our communications department, the local and national media, our radio and TV partners, and our community relations people. Not all of these meetings are positive or bring about happy outcomes. In fact, many of these meetings address issues that need immediate resolutions. By not letting myself have a bad day I was better able to deal with these situations and help the rest of the organization from over-reacting to the ebbs and flows that occur during a day.

I discovered that when I approached the challenges of the day with a positive, helpful attitude to serve others, it not only uplifted my spirits, but also set the tone for the entire organization and helped everyone perform at their highest levels. Keep in mind that your attitude is reflected in your body language, facial expressions, demeanor, and the inflection in your voice. The leaders of the team or organization set the tone and attitude. Every moment of the day someone on the team or organization is taking cues from you. A positive approach takes practice and a different mindset, but it's well worth the effort.

Contagious Leaders in the Locker Room

Mike Smith

I also witnessed the impact that a team member with a positive attitude can have on and off the field. I remember our first scrimmage, when our offensive coordinator Mike Mularkey and I were standing behind the huddle listening to rookie Matt Ryan call his first play. With the confidence of a seasoned quarterback, he told a veteran receiver that he was going to throw him the ball high and told him to go up and get it. Most first-year QBs don't think or talk with that much confidence. After the scrimmage, I looked at Mike and said, "It looks like we got ourselves a QB." Matt's positive attitude and approach to the game was contagious in other ways, too. He was always working to improve, whether it was during the season or the off-season. For example, Matt always had an off-season project that he felt was going to make him a better player. One year he studied the top five NFL quarterbacks in completion percentage and evaluated every throw that they had made the previous year. He wanted to see what they were doing and evaluate why they were so successful. The following season, he was in the top five in completion percentage. Another off-season, he was focused on gaining weight and getting stronger. He set the tone for the off-season by being the first player back in the weight room weeks before the off-season program officially started. When word got out that Matt had already started his off-season work in the weight room, it did not take long for the majority of the team to start their workouts prior to the official start date.

Matt's positive approach along with his contagious desire to be great rubbed off on the rest of the team and organization. No one ever worked harder than our starting quarterback, on and off the field. You have to have this type of leader and mentor on your team to maximize your chances of being successful. If you are fortunate to have a few team members with these traits who are embraced by the coaching staff and management, you will see it reverberate throughout the organization. This will help set and reinforce the expectations for the rest of the team and organization, and through this process, more players on your team and in your organization will become self-starters.

Tony Gonzales, a soon-to-be Hall of Famer, was also an incredible leader for us. There are different ways to be a contagious leader; some people are very vocal while others are quiet and let their actions speak. When Tony joined our team he had been one of the best players in the league and was arguably the greatest tight end to ever play. Tony was all about routine and he had a routine that he would go through before, during, and after practice to get in extra work. He would get out on the field about 15 minutes before practice started and work on catching passes. Almost every free minute that he had during the scheduled practice he would spend working the skill of catching the ball or refining his footwork coming out of breaks to improve his route running. It did not take long for others on the team to notice what Tony's routine was. As the days turned into weeks, almost the entire team started working on the specific skills of their positions during their free time in practice. They were mimicking what Tony was doing with his free time during practice. The receivers and quarterbacks had set their own routine to get extra work on catching the ball, and route running, and it was not unusual to see the different position groups working together on the specific skills they needed to be better players and teammates. Tony was a contagious leader who did not have to be verbal to lead. His quiet workmanlike approach spoke volumes and affected hundreds of players throughout his career.

When you talk about contagious leadership, you also have to talk about Ray Lewis, who I coached when I was with the Baltimore Ravens. Even though he has retired, Ray's legacy is a big reason why the Ravens still play great defense. His contagious attitude helped our defense hold the all-time NFL record for fewest points allowed in an NFL season. Ray was a very vocal, emotional, passionate leader of that team. His work ethic on and off the field was off the charts. Ray was all about accountability. First, he was always accountable to himself and then to the guy that lined up next to him. He always made sure that every member of the team understood that we were all relying on each other to be successful. Ray had this unbelievable love for what he was doing. He wanted to make sure that everyone around him was well prepared. He was a leader who developed leaders and mentored countless teammates who have gone on to be great players in their own right. Ray's attitude and his approach to preparation were so contagious in Baltimore that he inspired everybody to focus on the details of the weekly preparation before game day. I had never been around a group of players who were so prepared both physically and mentally to do their jobs on game day, and their commitment was because of Ray. He made everyone around him better.

In an ideal situation you would have one contagious leader or mentor in every position group on the team. Think of each position group as a separate department within an organization. The most successful teams that I have been around are the ones that have this contagious leadership and mentoring in each position group.

If you want to be successful, you must have contagious leaders like Matt Ryan, Tony Gonzalez, Ray Lewis, Mike Peterson, Marcus Stroud, Rod Woodson, Brian Finneran, and Trent Dilfer in your locker room. Your culture will come to life through the leaders and people in your locker room. Make sure you have the right team members to strengthen your culture instead of people who suck the energy out of it. You can do everything right as a leader and coach, but if you don't have positive mentors and team members in the locker room your culture and team will fall apart.

No Energy Vampires Allowed

Jon Gordon

I love Mike's stories about the impact a positive leader can have, and he nailed it when he talked about the detrimental impact a negative team member can have. A negative coach can sabotage the entire team's performance. He can give his team the gift of belief or the curse of doubt. We also know that one negative teammate can sabotage a team. One person can't make a team but one person can break a team. To build a positively contagious team you must not only feed the positive with a positive vision, belief, and attitude but you must also weed the negative from your team. You must literally post a sign that says "No Energy Vampires Allowed" and tell your team that you will not allow negativity to sabotage the vision you have and the team you expect to become. Mark Richt, head football coach at the University of Georgia, did this and the impact was powerful.

Four years ago, Mark called after visiting with Mike Smith and told me that his team was reading *The Energy Bus* and asked if I would speak to them. I spoke before the season, and unfortunately they lost their first two games. Georgia had been underperforming the previous few seasons and the media was reporting that Mark was on the hot seat and would lose his job if this season didn't go well. I texted him after the second loss and said "I believe in this team. I believe you all are going to turn it around." Mark texted me back and said, "Jon, the guys are still on the bus. In years past we've allowed energy vampires to ruin this team but not this year. This year we won't allow it." In the team meeting room, Mark had an artist draw a large picture of an energy vampire on the wall facing the seats where the players sit. If a player or coach acted like an energy vampire, the team took his picture and put it on the wall. No one wanted to be on the wall. It was a message from Mark to his team that they would stay positive through their adversity and challenges. It worked and the team went on to win the next 10 games in a row and made it to the SEC championship.

I shared this story with the University of Tennessee football team this past season and, when I was finished speaking, coach Butch Jones told the guys the meeting was over but then called out the names of 10 guys and told them to stay. I asked Butch who these guys were and he said, "Oh, these are our energy vampires."

I said, "Oh, you are going to deal with that now?"

He said, "Yes. Why wait?" After the meeting Butch walked out of the room and into the hallway where I was speaking to the athletic director. I asked him how it went. He said, "Powerful. Most of the guys admitted they were being energy vampires and are committed to being a positive influence on our team. They are going to be difference makers for us this season. But a few of the guys don't get it, won't change, and we will have to let them off the bus."

Tennessee overcame a lot of adversity that season and made their first bowl game in years. They were a great example that a team that stays positive together wins together. I'll never forget Butch's words: "Why wait?" To build a winning team you must create a positive culture where negativity can't breed and grow, and the sooner you start weeding it from your team the stronger and more positively contagious your culture and team will be.

The No Complaining Rule

Mike Smith

When it comes to weeding the negativity from your team you must also weed the subtle sources like complaining in addition to overt negativity like energy vampires. While it's obvious who your energy vampires are, complaining can often grow undetected beneath the surface and, if left to breed and grow, it can have disastrous effects on your team as well. That's why after reading Jon's book *The No Complaining Rule* I created a No Complaining Training Camp. The entire team was given the book for their summer reading and I gave the guys bracelets with "No Complaining" on them and told the team that they weren't allowed to complain. If they had a complaint they could bring it to me if they also had a suggested solution to the complaint. We were going to be a positive team who stayed upbeat through the long, hot August weather in Atlanta. We were not going to be a group of guys who complained about insignificant issues. It worked so well we declared it the No Complaining Season and our players wore the bracelets all the way through. Many members of the organization continue to wear them. I have worn mine for more than five years. I had players who asked me for additional bracelets so that they could give them to their immediate and extended family. We also had different departments (e.g., the marketing group and all the yearly interns) within the organization read the book and they wore the bracelets as well. It was a great tool and had a positive impact on our team. Guys would catch themselves complaining and stop. They realized that complaining is toxic to the team and locker room. I have found that a positive locker room helps create positive performance on the field.

What we think matters. Our words are powerful. Our body language is always being evaluated. The energy we share with our teammates and co-workers is essential. Instead of complaining, we focused on gratitude and appreciation for the chance to compete, to play a game we love, and the opportunity to get better. If you are complaining, you are not leading. If you are leading, you are not complaining. Great leaders are positively contagious and I encourage you to spend more time sharing a positive vision, belief, attitude, and encouragement with your team. If you do this you won't allow yourself to have a bad day and you'll give yourself and your team a better chance to have a great day.

Chapter 3

Consistent

*If you are not consistent,
you will lose the trust
your team has in you.
When you lose trust,
you lose the locker room.*

Consistency Wins the Locker Room

Mike Smith

 I see it all too often. Coaches will begin the season with one philosophy and attitude, only to change their approach and attitude when the team starts to lose. As a leader you must be consistent in your leadership style, approach, attitude, philosophy, and tactics. If you start off being supportive and friendly with players, you can't go from being a players' coach to someone everyone hates. You can't go from encouraging to condescending. If you are not consistent throughout the year you will lose your team's trust, and as soon as that happens, you lose the locker room and in turn lose games. Please know this doesn't mean you won't have moments of anger or frustration. We all do. If you are a coach with high expectations who yells at times, your team will know that's your style and they will expect that from you. The key is to be who you are and coach the way you do all year long no matter what your win–loss record is. Your team must know what to expect from you. They must see that you stick to your principles and philosophy through adversity and challenges. You must be the same coach at 0-8 as you are

8-0. It's hard to do, especially when you are losing and the pressure mounts, but if you don't, then you are doomed for failure. The character you possess during the drought is what your team will remember during the harvest.

Consistency Wins in the Long Run

Jon Gordon

A good friend of mine, Tom Flick, played quarterback for Joe Gibbs and the Washington Redskins. Most people don't remember that the Redskins were really bad when Joe took over the team, and they started the season 0-5 Joe's first year as head coach. Tom told me that when they lost their fifth game, the guys thought Joe was going to let them have it in the locker room after the game. They all gathered as coach prepared to address the team. The guys expected a tirade but Joe Gibbs said, "Men, we are getting closer." He encouraged them and focused on the process just as he had done all training camp and all season long. He was consistent and guided the Redskins to an 8-8 record that year and ultimately to three Super Bowls.

Examples like Joe Gibbs are great but the fact is being consistent isn't easy. Challenging situations, daily stress, and distractions can knock us off track. It's easy to lose our way. As a leader I want to encourage you to heed the advice of Pete Carroll, who when asked by my friend Rod Olson to describe his greatest challenge said, "My greatest challenge right now is to be consistent myself. I must be the 'same guy' all the time. I must be relentless in my pursuit of being consistent. I must discipline myself to be fully present so I can be in the moment with each person or player. Then we have a chance to maximize the moment together. My challenge is to be so consistent and optimistic, that every person in the organization feels that tomorrow will be better than today and we expect it to be."

It's Not Okay to Be Moody

Jon Gordon

It's not just the coaches who must be consistent, but each team member as well. One time I was visiting a college women's basketball team and they told me how they would often have to send one of the players home because she was in a bad mood and negatively affected the team. I asked if they had to do this with other players and they said there were several who were sent home occasionally. I then asked if these players were always in a bad mood. The coaches told me that they were positive sometimes and negative sometimes. Their moods fluctuated. They never knew what to expect and neither did their teammates. When I spoke to the team that day I told them that it was important for them to be consistent. I challenged them to be positively contagious. I told them point blank that's it's not okay to be moody. When you are moody, people around you don't know what to expect from you and this causes them to lose trust in you. I told them that no matter what is going on with school or your personal life, when you walk into the locker room you have to decide to impact your teammates in a positive way. To build a winning team, you want to be consistent in your attitude, effort, and actions. Have a great attitude all the time so you can give your best in everything you do. Focus on becoming the best version of yourself every day. Don't change with the wind; instead, be like a strong-rooted tree that does not waver, regardless of what is happening around it. Be the kind of leader everyone knows they can trust and count on.

Be Consistent in Your Desire to Be Great

Mike Smith

The greatest players I have coached have a consistent desire to be great. I have had the privilege to work with some of the best coaches and players in the world. The best of the best always have this one trait: the desire to be great. Your desire is measured by your routine and preparation. Ray Lewis had a driving desire to be the greatest linebacker to ever play. His daily, weekly, and yearly preparation was so detailed. His commitment to this process was unmatched by any other player. He was all in. He did everything in his power to be as prepared as he possibly could be. He would leave no stone unturned. Ray raised the level of performance of everyone that he came in contact with in the organization.

Jack Del Rio was the same way as a player and coach. I worked on the same coaching staff with Jack in Baltimore and served as his defensive coordinator in Jacksonville. Jack was a very good player in the NFL before starting his coaching career. Some people described Jack as an overachiever as a player. He played for 11 years and was named to the Pro Bowl in 1994. Call it what you want, but I call it being successful and sustainable. We would often have discussions when we were on the staff with the Ravens about what were the players' mindsets at different times of the year. Knowing that would help with the planning of the schedule throughout the year. As the head coach of the Jaguars, Jack would share with the team the importance of setting and following a routine throughout the season. He talked about his routine as a player and gave suggestions on how to prepare yourself both physically and mentally for the grind of an NFL season. It was a framework that had worked well for him and other players in the league. He shared the importance of following the routine and being consistent in your preparation. Jack knew that if you wanted to be great, you had to have a consistent routine that prepared you to be great. It was a powerful message he shared with his team and one that I often shared with mine.

As a head coach one of my priorities was to make sure my teams maintained this same desire to be great. Unfortunately, I feel like I let our team and organization become somewhat complacent in 2013. We had this feeling that we would be successful no matter what we did, forgetting about all the little things it took us to be successful the previous years.

Complacency Is a Disease

Mike Smith

Every team and organization must guard against the disease of complacency. It can be very subtle in its early stages. In fact it can go almost unnoticed. It is imperative that the leader of the organization not allow the seeds of complacency to germinate within the team. If they do, complacency will multiply faster than the most invasive weed. You become complacent when team members start to believe that their prior successes are going to ensure that they will have success in the future. In the case of the 2013 Falcons team, we lost sight of how the other teams in the NFL were trying to displace us as one of the top teams of the previous five seasons. We stopped focusing on the process as a team and organization. We ended up the season with a 4-12 record, when we had finished the previous season hosting the NFC Championship game. This was inexcusable, and as the head coach I was responsible. The NFL is a no-excuses business. You cannot blame it on factors outside of your control (e.g., injuries, bad breaks, etc.). Instead of allowing the guys to think they were going to automatically get back to the playoffs, the NFC Championship game, and even the Super Bowl, I should have done what I had done in previous years: create more urgency, focus on our desire to be great, identify what we need to do to improve, and most importantly focus on the process, not the outcome.

The difference between winning and losing in the NFL is truly a matter of inches—five or six plays in every game. Most business environments are highly competitive as well. Complacency has led to the demise of many teams, organizations, and companies because they were not looking forward and instead rested on their laurels while their competitors were doing everything in their power to overtake them. At the end of each year, you must go through an extensive evaluation of the entire organization to identify what you did well and where you fell short of your expectations. The most important aspect of this exercise is to identify how you are going to make sure that you are going to innovate and improve in the future. When you focus on the process instead of the destination, you make your desire to be great your number-one priority, so you won't allow the disease of complacency to set in. Being consistently complacent is something you definitely don't want. What you do want is consistent improvement, consistent coaching, and a consistent desire to be great.

Consistently Improving

Jon Gordon

The lesson Mike just shared is critical. Even the best coaches and teams can make the mistake of focusing on the past instead of creating the future. Bill Walsh, one of the greatest football coaches of all time, would often say that he feared success—not failure. He worried that once a player or team had success they would become complacent and stop striving to get better. He saw it too many times. A team would win a championship or a player would have a great season and then they would think that all they had to do was step on the field and they would automatically achieve the same results the following year, not realizing that it is the hard work, passion, and constant and consistent improvement that results in success. Each year the best recommit themselves to being better than they were the year before. The fact is, past success does not determine future success. Future success is the result of how you work, prepare, and practice and how you strive to improve each day. It's a commitment that the best of the best make every week, every day, every hour, and every moment. You have to consistently improve if you want to win consistently.

Humble and Hungry

Jon Gordon

Two words that characterize a team that is always improving and growing are "humble" and "hungry." Whether you are a team trying to become a winner or you have achieved the pinnacle of success, it's important to remember the following:

Be Humble

- Don't think you know it all. See yourself as a life-long learner who is always seeking ways to learn, grow, and improve.

- See everyone, including your competition, as teachers and learn from everyone.

- Be open to new ideas and strategies to take your work and team to the next level.

- When people tell you that you are great, don't let it go to your head. (And when they tell you that you stink, don't let it go to your head.)

- Live with humility because the minute you think you have arrived at the door of greatness it will get shut in your face.

- Remember that today's headlines are tomorrow's fish wrap.

Be Hungry

- Seek out new ideas, new strategies, and new ways to push yourself and your team out of your comfort zone.

- Be willing to pay the price that greatness requires. Don't be average. Strive to be great.

- Become the hardest working team you know.

- Love the process and you'll love what the process produces.

- Make your life and work a quest for excellence. Every day ask how can I be better today than I was yesterday?

- Don't rest on past laurels. Make your next work your best work.

Chapter 4

Communicate

When there is a void in communication,
negativity will fill it.
Fill the void with great communication.

The Most Important Thing a Coach Can Do

Jon Gordon

 I was having dinner with Doc Rivers, the head coach of the Los Angeles Clippers, and I asked him what was the most important thing he does as a coach. He said, "I communicate to my team. Not just collect-ively as a team but individually. I have to know where each person is in order to lead them where I need them to be. Since I communicate often with them, I know who is struggling with a personal issue. I know who needs encourage-ment. I know who needs to be challenged." I then asked Doc what he would like to improve upon as a coach. He said, "I would like to improve my communication." I was blown away. Here was a coach who was considered by many as the best communicator in sports and he wanted to get even better. It demonstrates how important communication is and how much every leader needs to focus on it.

Communication is the foundation of every great relation-ship. Communication builds trust. Trust generates commitment. Commitment fosters teamwork, and teamwork delivers results. Without great communication you don't have the trust to build a strong relationship. And without strong relationships you can't have a strong team. In fact, most marriages break down because of poor communication. Most teams break down because of poor communication. I have found that where there is a void in communication, negativity will fill it. Without great communication, negativity fills the void and it breeds and grows, resulting in negative contagious energy that quickly spreads. The key is to follow Doc Rivers' advice and make communication a huge priority. When you do, you'll realize that relationships are the foundation upon which winning teams are built and communication begins the relationship developing process. Having worked with Mike Smith all these years, one of the things I admire most about him as a leader is the way he communicates with his team. Even though he wouldn't tell you this, one of the popular phrases you hear from his players and all who know him is "Everyone loves Smitty" (that's his nickname). One of the reasons why they love him is because he communicates so well, and now you can hear from him in his own words how he does it.

One-on-One Communication

Mike Smith

I love what Doc Rivers told Jon about communication. It resonates deeply because communication is one of the key foundations of my leadership style and philosophy. As I mentioned earlier in the book, when I first took over as head coach I met with everyone in the organization and also with each member of my team. In the basketball world you only have 12 to 20 players. However, in football you have a larger team and it makes communication much more challenging. But if you want to win in the locker room and on the field or court, you have to do it.

When I became head coach, during the first 45 days or so, while Thomas and our staffs were working to calibrate the roster it was important to meet with as many players on the roster as possible. This was a team that had three different head coaches in a period of 12 months. The coach before me resigned before the season was over. The players felt abandoned, and to say trust was lacking would be an understatement. The meetings with the players were spread out over a three-week period. It was very time consuming, but it was the best way to learn about the culture and the other dynamics that were impacting the team on and off the field. I also wanted to get feedback on why the Falcons had struggled with consistency, so I asked the same questions of each player:

- Do we have the players on the roster to be a playoff team?
- Is there a burning desire on the team to be the best that they could possibly be?
- If not, why do you see it that way?
- Is the team a group of men that enjoy being around each other?
- Is this a group of individuals who happen to wear the same colored jersey and helmet or a team?
- Are the guys on the team having fun?
- When you were not getting the results that you wanted, how did the players deal with it?

53

Communicate

- Do they take responsibility or do they point the finger at others?

While these types of questions often make people uncomfortable and usually result in politically correct answers, I was looking for honest, engaging dialogue from guys who wanted to get better—and thankfully I found it. One of the best conversations I had was with Todd McClure (nicknamed Mud Duck), a seventh round draft pick in 1999 who had been the starting center since 2000. Mud Duck was a no-nonsense veteran player who from the very first meeting was transparent and shared his views on why the Falcons had struggled in years past. He and a handful of other veterans were really instrumental in helping Thomas and I address some of the issues that had affected the Falcons negatively in years past. The conversations and communication with our team were some of the most important things we did to rebuild the Falcons. It created the pathway to stronger relationships and a much stronger team.

Please know that I realize it's not easy to consistently have one-on-one communication with everyone in the organization. I realize you can't meet with everyone all the time, especially if you lead a large organization. The key is to meet with your leadership team and the people you lead directly, and then make sure they are communicating well with the people they lead. If everyone does this throughout the organization, relationships, teamwork, and performance will improve dramatically. I'm also a big believer in having an open-door policy to encourage interaction and let everyone know that you are always available to talk. This lets your team know that you are always there for them, and when you make the time and effort to communicate with them it comes back to you tenfold. Besides, the only way to really get to know your team and have them know you is to interact with them one on one.

Listening Enhances Communication

Mike Smith

People often think of communication as talking, but for me it's all about listening. The best communicator is not the person who is the most eloquent speaker, but the person who has the ability to listen, process the information, and use it to make decisions that are in the best interest of the team and organization. The best listeners truly hear what a person is saying and trying to convey.

An example of listening that really made a difference for our team happened in one of our over-30 club meetings (for players age 30 and older). This group of players on the team had the most experience in the NFL and they were leaders and mentors. We would have four to six meetings throughout the year to discuss how our team was functioning, and it was a great time to listen to the challenges we were facing, learn more about one another, and listen to new ideas from the players' perspective. During the season in 2010, we had a discussion about our daily in-season schedule. The players wanted to start our workday a few minutes later in the morning and shorten the amount of time between our morning session on the field and the afternoon practice. The group had a number of compelling reasons for the adjustments. I listened and heard what they were saying. Their point of view on the sequence of the practice day had merit and their suggestions were discussed with the coaching staff. We incorporated the changes they suggested into our daily schedule, and doing so helped us operate with much more efficiency on and off the field. We started to play our best football of the season and were a team that was well rested as we headed into the playoffs that year. When you listen and hear what your team members are saying, you open the lines of communication and develop a team that is "all in." Your team feels heard and buys in to your leadership because they know and feel that they are a part of the process of building and sustaining success.

One of the keys to listening and communicating is to ask the right people the right questions. For example, each week I would visit with Matt Ryan to make sure that he felt comfortable with the offensive game plan. I wanted to be certain that he felt great about it and was confident that every play on the call sheet was going to work. If he didn't, I would get his input and suggestions and discuss them with our offensive coordinator and offensive staff. It was important to get feedback from Matt and other key members of the team. While doing this we made sure we were looking at game plans from different perspectives and coming up with the best strategies that utilized his and our team's strengths to win. It also let Matt know that I was in his corner and would do whatever it took to help him be successful. One of the most important relationships in football is the one between the head coach and the quarterback, and Matt and I developed a great relationship that continues to this day. It didn't start with me talking. It started with me asking questions and listening. Of course, I also made sure I asked questions and listened to my coaches and coordinators. They knew I communicated with both them and the players. By doing so I was able to learn a lot more, which led to more questions and more helpful answers. As a head coach you must trust your coordinators and not micromanage, but you must also question them and question your team to ultimately make the best decisions. Just as Abraham Lincoln would ask his advisors questions and receive different ideas and competing strategies before eventually making his decisions, coaches and all leaders must do the same.

What's the Temperature Today?

Mike Smith

To be the most effective leader possible, you have to take the temperature of the building. I am not talking about what the thermostat reads. I am talking about the pulse of the team and the energy in the building. Oftentimes leaders will only concern themselves with the temperature of the organization when things are not going well. This can be a big miscalculation. It is just as important to know what the vibes are when things are going well.

In athletics the pulse can be different every day based on the result of the previous game, the day of the week, the practice schedule, or the news cycle. It can change in the off-season as the roster is being calibrated, and fluctuate during the playoffs as the pressure mounts. The dynamics of an organization, whether in sports or business, are always changing and as the leader, you have to be prepared to manage the ebbs and flows that occur by taking the temperature each day. Having an accurate assessment of the mood of the building at all times will allow you to make the best decisions for your team or organization.

To do this you want to use all the resources that are available to get a read on the building. You don't want to just rely on a few leaders and decision makers to get your information. Players will act differently in the presence of the head or assistant coach than they will if the coach or supervisor is not around. The best way to gauge the temperature is to have different "thermostats" around the building. Members of the training staff, equipment managers, communications staff, and the player development team are invaluable. I would literally walk around and ask these people, "What's the temperature today?" and they would share priceless information. I became aware of many different situations, both positive and negative, by asking what the temperature was and having these conversations. I found out from the equipment staff that one of our players was really angry about something. I discovered from the training staff that one of our players was having off-field challenges. I learned of internal conflicts between players. I listened and heard that certain players were really pessimistic after a loss. By asking what the temperature was I not only learned more about the team but I also engaged different people throughout the organization and reinforced the fact that they were part of the process of being the best organization possible. This helped our organization operate at the highest level and deal with potentially negative issues before they impacted our culture and performance.

As a leader you can't just speak to other leaders who have a similar vantage point as you. You have to engage people who are closest to the potential challenges facing your organization. You have to ask questions, listen, and learn, and then decide how to use the readings to make decisions going forward.

Leading by Walking Around

Mike Smith

A big part of taking the temperature of the building is leading by walking around. You can't make great decisions by sitting in your office. The most effective leaders are the ones who are mobile and visible throughout the building, not just in the office but also in the training room, locker room, and cafeteria. You lead by leaving a footprint in every area of the building. When you interact with your team and organization all over the building you break down that separation of upstairs and down-stairs, office and locker room.

Each day I made a couple of trips to the training room to visit with players who were getting treatment. When players are in the training room during the season, they fall into one of four categories. The first is that they are injured to the extent that they will not be able to play anymore this season. The second is that they are definitely out for the upcoming game or longer. The third is that they are injured and have a chance to play in the upcoming game. The fourth is that they are receiving maintenance treatment and will be available to play. I always wanted them to know that regardless of their individual situation I was concerned and interested in how they were doing, regardless of their practice status. Some of the best conversations I have had with players have taken place in the training room.

The visits to the weight room were of equal importance. It let them know the work that they were doing with the athletic performance department was a huge part of the success of the organization. In fact, depending on the time of year, assistant coaches and members of the personnel staff would be using the weight room at the same time. This was just another way to strengthen the culture and communication in the organization.

The cafeteria is another opportunity to have conversations with the players in a different setting. Sitting down and having a meal with someone allows for conversations to take place in a more comfortable atmosphere. I learned a lot and developed great relationships with my players just by talking to them during meals.

And of course I spent a lot of time in the locker room. I would often walk in and just look around to see who was talking to who, what the energy was like, and what the overall mood of the team was. I felt that these different views of the building were essential. If you make visits to these different areas, you will be amazed by what you will find out. You will be able to feel the pulse of the team and learn who is connecting and what potential issues are arising. Once the issues are identified, you can confront them before they become bigger problems that can sabotage the team dynamic. I realized that a big part of winning in the locker room is making sure you know what's going on down there and shaping the team and culture before it shapes you.

Communicating the Message

Mike Smith

Beyond one-on-one communication, a big part of any coach's job is to share key messages, themes, and principles with your team. Each year we had a theme for the season that we presented to the team during the off-season. We would also have weekly themes and messages that were presented at the Wednesday team meeting and were applicable to the upcoming game. While there are many ways in which you can present the yearly and weekly messages, it's critical to make sure that you drive the message home the first time you present it. Then, after the first presentation, you want to make sure you reinforce the themes and messages over and over again, almost until they become annoying to the players. You have to say them so often that they become ingrained in their minds. You want these themes and messages at the forefront of the thoughts of every player, coach, and member of the organization for the entire season.

It is also essential that your leadership team (in my case it was the assistant coaches) also share and reinforce the same messages with the team. The message can't come from only one person and you can't have different messages coming from different leaders. Every leader in the organization must be echoing the same beliefs and sharing the same message, especially the mentors and leaders in the locker room. The message must be consistent both in spoken words and actions. Coaches and leaders can't just talk about the message, they must model the message. If you don't live it, neither will your team. But if you are consistent with your messages in words and deeds you will build trust and strengthen your culture and team. Consistent messaging is essential to a team's success.

People often ask me how a leader knows if the message is getting through and I tell them it's simple: You know that the message was accepted by the team when you hear it being talked about in the locker room, on the practice field, in the cafeteria, the training room, and to the media. I loved it when I would hear a player in an interview on television echo the message we had been consistently reinforcing. When the message becomes something that you are hearing from the players over and over again in the media, then you know that they have bought in and are *all in*.

One of the ways we would present a theme for the season was by presenting "challenge coins" to the players and coaches. This was something we also did for the defensive players in Jacksonville when I was the defensive coordinator. Dave Campo, who was the former head coach of the Dallas Cowboys and longtime assistant coach in the league, was the one who came up with the idea and we started doing it in 2005. One year in Jacksonville the theme for the year was "mastering the fundamentals of your job and playing with unity on the defense." That year we had the best season, statistically, out of Dave's and my entire tenure with the Jaguars. The reason behind our success was that we played as a unit and each player's focal point was to be the most fundamentally sound team in the NFL. In Atlanta during my first season in 2008, the theme was to "embrace the process." That was the messaging that was given over and over to the players, fans, and media. It was quite amusing when members of the media started likening it to a buzzword because you heard it from everybody in the building at our complex in Flowery Branch. You could tell they were almost bored with the interviews because we said the same thing over and over again. They wanted more, but that's all they got. They didn't like it but I did. That is when you know that message was driven home. Mission accomplished.

The Power of an Outside Voice

Jon Gordon

To add to Mike's thoughts about communicating your message to your team, it's also key to have outside voices reinforce the messages and themes that you are sharing. I once had a CEO say to me, "Jon, never underestimate the power of an outside voice." I had just spoken at his company's annual meeting and he said, "We brought you here to reinforce our message. Our folks get tired of hearing us say it, but when it comes from an outside voice it's new, fresh, and exciting." I knew exactly what he was talking about. My kids have little interest in what I have to say. From what many parents tell me, I know I'm not alone. So, besides writing inspirational messages on whiteboards in my children's rooms, I've resorted to outside voices to reinforce the message and principles I want to share with them. I have found coaches, tutors, mentors, experts, and others to encourage, coach, teach, challenge, and bring out the best in my children. There's something about the power of an outside voice and it's beneficial to use a few to share and reinforce important principles and messages with your team. The more times they hear it, from different people, in different ways and styles, the

63

more it will resonate. Videos, books, music, and speakers are great resources to tap and share with your team.

The Enemies of Great Communication

Jon Gordon

If you are like me and most leaders you'll realize after reading this section that you need to do a better job of communicating with your team. You know you fall short but you are not quite sure why. Well, we would be remiss if we didn't share with you the enemies that prevent us from communicating well. You see, you can have the best intentions in the world to communicate with your team and create a communication plan; however, if you don't deal with the busyness and stress that sabotage your communication, your team will suffer. When you are busy and stressed you activate the reptilian part of your brain. The reptile is all about survival and so are you when you are busy and stressed. When you activate the reptile, you don't think about communicating with others and developing relationships. Your only focus is your own survival. So you spend each day merely trying to get through the day and survive instead of helping your team thrive. The key is to be aware that these enemies exist, take a deep breath, slow down, and make communication a priority. Other things may be urgent but remind yourself that communication is what matters. Research says that you can't be stressed and thankful at the same time. So breathe, practice gratitude, and in the midst of busyness find mindful moments of calm to make communication and connection happen. You and your team will be glad you did.

Communication Must Lead to Collaboration

Mike Smith

The first head coach that I worked for in the NFL was Brian Billick, and he was the best communicator that I have ever been around. He was a great listener and encouraged conversations and even debates between the staff and the players. It was these conversations that not only led to great game plans each week but also to a feeling of inclusion among staff and players. When staff members and players are included, they take ownership of the process. When you have buy-in during the week—from everyone involved in planning and implementing the game plan—you eliminate the second guesses that can emerge after a loss. That's why I communicated with key players like Matt, Roddy, Julio, Spoon, Brook, Osi, and Kroy each week, in addition to my coordinators and coaches.

After winning the 2000 Super Bowl, the Baltimore Ravens' staff had three assistants (in addition to me) who went on to be successful head coaches in the NFL: Marvin Lewis with the Cincinnati Bengals; Jack Del Rio, first with the Jacksonville Jaguars and now the Oakland Raiders; and Rex Ryan, first with the New York Jets and now the Buffalo Bills. In Baltimore, Marvin Lewis was the defensive coordinator. We had a very good staff and arguably one of the best defenses in the history of the NFL. Marvin was the coach who called the plays for the defense. On game day he was the absolute best I have been around. He would call an almost flawless game and put our team in great situations to make plays. Marvin had a way about him that included everybody on the defensive staff in the process of putting together the game plan. Brian had created

65

Communicate

the structure that encouraged the communication and Marvin implemented it with the defensive staff and players.

In addition to coaching their position groups, every member of the defensive staff had specific responsibilities for presenting to the rest of the staff and players in meetings. As an assistant you took ownership of the area you presented. If you were responsible for short yardage and goal line you took it personally if we did not play well in those situations. This collaboration not only helped us work better together, it also prepared us to become future coordinators and head coaches.

This structure also included involving the players. The players' perspective is important because they are the ones who will have to go out and execute the specific plays the defensive coordinator calls. You want the players to have confidence in the defensive calls and there is no better way than to encourage them to have input into the game plan.

During my time with Baltimore and Jacksonville and my years with the Falcons, I became increasingly convinced that it's not just communication that helps a team be successful, but rather the collaboration that follows. Communication without collaboration can lead to underperformance, but when you have a collaborative team that works closely together in an effort to be great, you produce something very special. Collaborative teams and organizations are also much better prepared to deal with the ever-changing dynamics that are caused by both internal and external factors. So don't just communicate—make sure you and your team are also collaborating to be your best.

Chapter 5

Connect

Team beats talent when talent isn't a team.

Communicating and Collaborating Leads to Connection

Jon Gordon

 A great benefit of communicating and collaborating is that they develop connections between you and your team members. Communication begins the process of building trust, collaboration fosters this process and enhances relationships, and this leads to stronger connections between team members. This is crucial because when you have stronger connections, you have a more committed and powerful team. A connected team becomes a committed team.

The more I have worked with teams over the years, the more I realize that connection is the *key* to becoming a great team. And a lack of connection between team members leads to below-average teamwork and sub-par performance and results. Connection is the difference between a team that thrives and one that and crumbles. One of the biggest complaints I receive from coaches is that their teams aren't connected. They have a bunch of young men or women who usually focus on themselves, their personal goals, their social media followings, and their egos. They usually have family and friends telling them they should be playing more, scoring more, or getting more recognition. The message they receive from the world is that it's all about the individual, not the team. It's about me, not we. This creates a disconnect between personal goals and team goals, and it undermines the team. I have found that when coaches and players focus on becoming a connected team, the *me* dissolves into *we*. The individual silos come crumbling down, bonds are strengthened, relationships are developed, and the team becomes much more connected, committed, and stronger.

Team Beats Talent When Talent Isn't a Team

Jon Gordon

Before the 2013–14 college basketball season, I received a call from Billy Donovan, the former University of Florida basketball coach who is now the head coach of the Oklahoma City Thunder. Billy shared the challenges his team was facing and asked for my advice. I shared the 7 C's with him and Billy immediately zoomed in on connection. He said, "That's it, Jon. We often get to the Elite Eight but have trouble pushing through to the Final Four because we aren't as connected as we need to be. If we are more connected, we will have a better chance of winning the tight, big games." Billy and I kept in touch during the season and I was blown away by all he did to connect with his players and foster relationships between them. I never saw a coach do more to invest in a team than what Billy did that season. The walls came crumbling down and instead of a group of individuals the Florida team became a connected family.

They pushed through the Elite Eight to the Final Four and beat a very talented Kentucky team three times that season. Despite the fact that not one person on their team was drafted into the NBA, Florida was able to beat teams with more talent because they were more connected. They are a great example of how team beats talent when talent isn't a team. You may not have the most talented players, but if you are a connected team you will beat many talented teams who lack a close bond.

I saw the same phenomenon on the University of Nebraska basketball team that same season. I spoke to all the school's athletes and coaches that January after the basketball season had already started. The Nebraska team was having an average season and after my talk, where I shared the importance of being a connected team, I had lunch with coach Tim Miles. We talked about ways to become more connected and Tim focused on improving the connections and positivity of his team thereafter. They went on to have a great season, making it to the NCAA tournament for the first time in years. I truly believe when a coach and team connect with each other, commitment, teamwork, chemistry, and performance improve dramatically.

We Got This

Mike Smith

I've seen the power of a connected team many times in my coaching career. The Ravens' 2000 Super Bowl team was the most connected team I have ever been associated with. This team was able to stay together through some very difficult times. We had one of the best defenses ever and set the all-time record for fewest points allowed in an NFL season. We gave up 165 points during the entire regular season. In our four playoff games we only gave up one defensive touchdown. This team also went through a stretch of five games without scoring an offensive touchdown. (We were only able to win two of those five games.)

It is not unusual for teams to have morale problems when one side of the team is performing at a high level and the other is not. This is when the blame game usually starts and can lead to a divided locker room and disconnected team. But that was not the case with the 2000 Ravens. Head Coach Brian Billick, with the help of veteran players like Rod Woodson, Ray Lewis, Tony Siragusa, and Rob Burnett did a great job of navigating the team through the five-week drought without an offensive touchdown. Brian was able to communicate with the leaders of the team and deal with all the different issues that were in play. He handled it with transparency, and even sometimes with humor so that our team would not get uptight. They made sure that there never was any finger pointing. The defensive players had so much confidence in themselves that they knew if the offense could kick a couple of field goals we were going to be alright and win the game. The defense focused only on what they could control and they were very supportive of the offense as they worked through the process of playing their way out of their slump. Going through that five-game stretch galvanized the team instead of sabotaging it. We knew that if we did not implode in this situation, we could handle anything that an opponent could throw at us. When you are connected you are able to turn your misfortune into fortune, and we did that.

The most connected team that I had in Atlanta was our 2012 team. The 2012 team had seven fourth-quarter or last-drive wins, and all of them occurred under completely different circumstances. The first come-from-behind victory of the season came in week four against the Carolina Panthers. The defense got a critical third and inches stop with 59 seconds remaining on the clock, and they were disciplined to not jump offside on fourth and inches while the Panthers attempted to draw them offside. The offense followed it up by moving the ball from the one-yard line with no time-outs to Carolina's 22-yard line. The drive got started with a big completion from Matt Ryan to Roddy White to move us off the shadow of our own goalpost. Matt Bryant and our special teams unit kicked the game winner with six seconds remaining.

This was the type of finish that we had become accustomed to in 2012, and we had to stay connected as a team to achieve the outcomes we had worked so hard for. We earned our way into the NFC Championship game by having our seventh come-from-behind victory of the year. After receiving the kickoff after going down by one point with 31 seconds remaining, our special teams unit came up with a big 35-yard return by Jacquizz Rodgers. After two quick completions of 19 and 22 yards to Tony Gonzalez and Harry Douglas, we had moved into field-goal range and kicked the game-winning field goal with six seconds left. The entire team and coaching staff contributed to all of these victories.

When you have these types of challenges throughout the season, it will test your resiliency as a team. It will also test your team's level of connectivity. When you are connecting as teammates, you reach a level of confidence that will take you a long way in overcoming the issues that can cause dysfunction within the team. This dysfunction can lead to underperformance on and off the field. The level of connectivity on this team was the driving force to our success in 2012. They knew that if we stayed together and battled through the ups and downs of the season and continually worked on staying connected, that we were always going to be in a position to get the outcome that we wanted. We knew that when it was time for someone to step up and make a game-changing play, that we would get it done. When your team is connected, you have this synergy within the organization that will not allow your team to disintegrate.

Unplug from Technology and Plug into People

Mike Smith

We live in a more connected world today than any time in history. The advancement in technology over the last 30 years definitely has made life easier in many ways. It has also made life more difficult in many ways too. I can remember when the computer was introduced to coaching and the many ways people expected it to be used in game planning. It was going to allow coaches to not have to spend long hours breaking down game video. It was going to make our jobs easier and less time consuming because of the ability to quickly evaluate and analyze data as we looked for tendencies in our opponents. Coaches were no longer going to have to work 16 to 18 hours during the season. This new technology definitely reduced the time we devoted to the analysis of opponents' tendencies, but it did not reduce the time that coaches were working. Faster analysis of the data and the ability to connect it to the digital video created the drive to get even more analytical data from the breakdowns. We could now slice and dice the data in so many different ways that we had to be careful to avoid analysis paralysis. The technology that is meant to help us can harm us if we let it. The same goes for our connected devices.

We have so many different ways that we can communicate with one another, but unfortunately we are connecting less meaningfully. We are designing machines that function like people and, in turn, are turning people into machines. I have seen a change over the last couple of years in regard to face-to-face interaction in the locker room. More guys are connecting with their devices than with each other. This became alarming as I saw team members missing opportunities to cultivate relationships. The best teams I have been around were teams that enjoyed being around each other. When you are a team that does not connect, you will be a team that fails to win.

When you are dealing with professional adults, it's difficult to tell them to put their phones away, but I do believe it's a topic that everyone should discuss. As a team you must recognize the importance of connecting with each other and identify ways you can make these connections happen. You might have a no-phone zone, or a no-phone time during road trips to encourage conversation. Some teams stay off social media during the season. Other teams allow it. Every team is going to be different and certain ideas will work for some teams and not others. The key is to agree on ways and times to unplug from technology and plug into each other.

Please know that I'm not anti-technology. I believe it's very valuable if utilized the right way. I don't think our mobile devices should be our main form of connecting with each other, but I do think they're a valuable way to connect as a supplemental form of communication. For example, as a coach, texting is a great way to share a word of encouragement or let a player know you are thinking about them and available to talk if they are facing a challenge. I heard that Mike "Coach K" Krzyzewski started texting his players this year, something he hadn't done before, and he even learned how to use Twitter. If Coach K is willing to use technology to connect with his college athletes, that says a lot. Young athletes today frequently communicate through devices and if coaches and leaders want to connect with them, we have to adapt and contact them in this way. However, it should be in addition to one-on-one conversations where you can look people in the eye and have a meaningful heart-to-heart and truly connect. This is where real relationships and connections are developed. Social media and texting simply allow you to develop and strengthen this connection if utilized the right way.

Create a Connected Locker Room

Jon Gordon

I love what Mike said about having heart-to-heart conversations, and I don't think you should wait to have them by chance. I believe that to create a connected team and locker room you have to make time to connect and plan activities that facilitate this. At home my family has a meeting once a week. If we didn't have this family meeting, we would probably never slow down enough to have the conversations we need to have and make the connections with each other that we need to make. We live in a world filled with busyness and stress, and when you are going through life at 100 miles per hour, the last thing you want to do is connect with people—but it's the most important thing you can do to build a great team. As a leader, you have to be intentional about connecting with your team and creating ways for team members to connect with each other. Many teams I work with at the college level bring in former Navy SEAL team-building experts who take a team through a series of exercises designed to foster bonds and connections. I've also worked with other teams that have utilized my books *The Energy Bus*, *Training Camp*, *One Word*, and *The Hard Hat* to foster connections. The entire team reads a book together and then discusses it. I've also heard about teams that present the principles from the book to each other in the form of skits, videos, poems, and so on. The team is divided into small groups of two or three people, and each group is responsible for presenting one of the rules in a creative way to the rest of the team.

A lot of teams I've spoken to have also done our one-word exercise where each team member chooses a word for the year and commits to living that word. It's very effective when team members share their word with each other and why they chose it. For example, a player for the Army basketball team chose the word *nails* because he wanted to be tough as nails. When he tore his ACL the team adopted *nails* as their team word. Countless Division 1 basketball and football programs have done this one-word exercise with powerful results. I even did it with Mike and the Atlanta Falcons the year they played in the NFL championship game.

I'm also a big believer in team-building exercises where team members can be vulnerable and share meaningful stories and feelings with each other. One of my favorite exercises is "Hero, Hardship, and Highlight." This is where team members share who their hero is, a highlight (great moment) in their life, and a hardship they had to face. As your team members share their stories, everyone connects in a meaningful way. I also love the "Defining Moment" exercise. This is where you go around the room and people share a defining moment in their life. When you learn about someone's defining moment, you get to know him or her a whole lot better. And my all-time favorite exercise is "If you really knew me, you would know *this* about me." When team members share with each other, their hearts open, the walls come crumbling down, and their vulnerability turns into connection and strength. Of course you have to make sure you create a *safe place* where everyone knows that everything shared is confidential and not to be shared with anyone outside of the team. These exercises work very well with college teams but may be more challenging with high school teams given their age and maturity level. Every human being has past moments of pain, hurt, and fear, and when you share your feelings you are able to heal and grow. When individuals grow and connect, teams become stronger. Vulnerability may seem weak, but in truth it is the pathway to meaningful connections and a powerful team. When team members connect and build strong relationships, they don't just work with each other. They work *for* each other.

Connect Outside the Locker Room to Be Strong Inside the Locker Room

Mike Smith

To truly connect as a team it's also important to connect outside the locker room. We purposefully tried to find opportunities for everyone on the team and in the organization to connect more frequently. For example, throughout the season we held functions that involved the players, coaches, scouts, and support staff and all of their families. We held family night dinners on Wednesdays when we were playing on the road so the kids had an evening to spend time with their dads. This also created a chance for us to be together as a large group in a non-workplace setting. We had different activities throughout the season based on holidays like Halloween, Thanksgiving, and Christmas. We also had a guest-chef program where different players were chosen to set the menu for lunch on Thursday in the second half of the season. The meal had to have a theme and the players would try to outdo one another. Some of the best "celebrity chef" meals we had were Todd McClure's Cajun menus and Jonathan Babineaux's Caribbean spreads. These are just a few ways to work on connecting outside of the locker room. As the leader of the team or organization you should always be looking for ways to enhance these types of connections.

We also wanted to create opportunities for the players to get together outside of the pressures of the workplace. Some of the activities that we had were tied to community service or fundraising events for local charities. It is easy to overlook how blessed we are, regardless of what our profession is. Giving back to our community and to the people who are less fortunate is another way to work on being a more connected team or organization. We tried to make these times fun and enjoyable for our players. We had events like Huddle Up for Miracles, where players were celebrity waiters and competed to see who could raise the most money through tips. We also supported programs like Feed the Hungry and Christmas shopping for families in need. We had planned golf and bowling events. I wanted the players to see how active we were as a team and posted the names of all the players who made appearances during the previous week at our team meeting on Wednesday. There were years when we would have over 1,000 community visits. One of my favorite events was our golf outing, which we called the Jocks versus the Hacks, where we played with the media and coaches.

These moments of connection really made a difference. When your team is connected, you will see and feel it in the way they treat each other. You will see players and staff interacting on many different levels. You will see players' and coaches' respect for one another grow, and the other people within the organization will tear down the proverbial walls in which people and departments typically operate. This is one of the leading indicators that you have a connected team. When you are a truly connected team you will see players participating together in the functions outside of the locker room. You will see players getting together for dinners, card games, worship services, golfing, bowling, and just enjoying time together. You will also see players supporting one another's philanthropic endeavors. I'm convinced this level of connectivity is what will take your team or organization to the top.

Stay Connected

Mike Smith

I told you that I was going to share some of the key lessons I have learned and this is a big one that I want you to take to heart. Once you develop a connection with your team members, it's important to make sure you stay connected. It's so easy to take your connection for granted. Looking back on my seven years with the Falcons, I realize that connection is something you must keep working on. The connections within the organization are never static, they are always changing. I now see it very clearly that Thomas and I weren't as connected at the end as we were in the beginning. Like a marriage ending too soon, you can think everything is fine but when you look back, you realize that you stopped working at it. Thomas and I always had a great relationship and still do, but what I think happens is that when you have worked with each other for so long and know each other so well, you begin to take things for granted. You assume that since we were connected in the past, we are still connected at the same level. You know the saying about what happens when you assume right? You cannot lose sight of the fact that every year it is a new and different staff and team. One thing for sure is that every year there are going to be different pieces that make up the team and organization. When the dynamics and makeup are always changing, you as the leader have to always evaluate how well we are connecting, who is connecting, and whether there is a positive or negative charge. I think it's easy to assume everything is fine, but when you look back, you realize you should have spent more time together discussing decisions, challenges, and issues that cause a team to fall short of its full potential.

It's all those little conversations that you had in the beginning that help you build a winning team, and you must force yourself to keep having those conversations regardless of whether you are winning or losing. Connection at the top of an organization is especially important. Teams that are not connected at the top crumble at the bottom. Do not underestimate the effect it will have if the leadership team's level of connectivity is not as strong as it had been in previous years.

Now, I can't change my past but I can help you create your future by encouraging you to stay connected as a leadership team. Stay connected with your players. Help your players stay connected with each other. The connection you create today will be the bond that strengthens your team tomorrow.

Chapter 6

Commitment

It's not about you.
It's about committing yourself to your team.

Commit if You Want Commitment

Mike Smith

 When talking to my team about commitment I like to tell them about the hen and pig and their roles in breakfast. The hen is involved in creating the eggs for breakfast, but the pig is committed. He has to sacrifice everything. To be a great leader, coach, and team member you must be more than involved. You must be committed. A leader must do a self-evaluation to make sure that his or her level of commitment is greater than that of anyone else in the organization. This commitment will come in many forms. You must commit to doing everything in your power to make sure you have created the right environment for your team to thrive, grow, improve, and enjoy the journey. You have to be committed to making your team better. You have to be prepared to make tough and sometimes unpopular decisions. You have to spend time developing your players' gifts and strengths. Everyone on the team and in the organization must see that commitment in your actions every day 24/7—it can't be a sometimes thing. It must be an all-the-time approach. You cannot have different levels of commitment based on how well the team is performing or how well an individual is performing. You have to show your team that you are willing to do whatever it takes to help them be the best they can possibly be regardless of their stage of growth. If you commit to helping each member of your team be the best version of him- or herself, over time this will lead to greater individual and team performance.

Commitment is something you should spend more time demonstrating than talking about. It shows in your actions, in how you treat people, and how you interact with every member of your team. When you are committed, everyone knows it and your team feels it. Coaches often want their teams to be committed, but there's no way you will get buy-in unless you demonstrate your commitment to them first. They have to know that you are there to serve, teach, and coach. They have to see, hear, and feel your commitment, and know that you want them to be just as successful off the field as they are on the field. You demonstrate this commitment each day with the time you give your team and your willingness to serve them and help them improve. When your team knows you are committed to helping them be their best they will then be committed to you and give their all for you.

Commitment Begins with the Leader

Mike Smith

One of the reasons why I took the job with the Atlanta Falcons was because I knew Arthur Blank, the team's owner, was a man who was committed to his team and to winning. In March of 2005, three years before I met Arthur, the NFL held a coaching symposium in Orlando, Florida, for selected assistant coaches. It was an opportunity for us to interact with owners, head coaches, and general managers, and a few of them did presentations on topics of interest. In Orlando, Arthur was one of the presenters, and because I had never met him, I did not know much about his background. When he was introduced, I became aware that he was the co-founder of Home Depot. Of course, I was familiar with Home Depot and was always impressed by how the associates in the stores were so helpful. They made it clear that they were there to serve the people who were shopping in the store and make sure that it was a great experience. I knew this commitment to service didn't begin on the front lines and in the stores; to have such committed employees, I knew Arthur had to be a man who believed in serving his team.

Years later, after a few years coaching the Falcons, I personally witnessed the legacy Arthur had left at Home Depot. I went with him to Home Depot headquarters for a function with our ticket and marketing group. The event was being held exclusively for all of the thousands of employees at Home Depot headquarters. Arthur was no longer the owner of the company, but he received a standing ovation from the group as he was introduced. It was his first time back in the building since leaving the organization, and, clearly, he was someone they remembered fondly and admired for his service. Commitment begins at the top.

Feeling Is More Powerful than Hearing

Jon Gordon

When I visited West Point in the summer of 2014, the USA basketball team happened to be visiting at the same time.

Head coach Mike "Coach K" Krzyzewski brought the team there to understand what it truly means to represent the United States of America. Coach K knew the place was special. After all, he attended West Point, played basketball there under Bob Knight, returned as the head coach after his five years of military service, and coached there for five years before becoming the head coach of Duke University. Coach K knew the players wouldn't fully understand how special the place was by hearing him talk about it. They had to experience and feel it. He said, "You can't talk about this place, see a movie about this place, you have to feel this place. You go to a place like this, you get it."

Coach K knew it was the same when talking about service and sacrifice. The players had to feel it, so at the beginning of their visit, Coach K brought the team to the West Point Cemetery, where they had a meeting with family members of fallen soldiers. The players on Team USA listened as the family members told them about their children and how they died serving their country. The players may have understood the concept of service and sacrifice before, but after seeing the graves of the fallen soldiers, listening to personal stories of service and sacrifice, and feeling the loss of the family members, they truly got it. It's also a powerful lesson for all of us. Feeling is more powerful than hearing. Your team must feel your commitment. Not just hear it. When we hear from a leader, we will learn; but when we feel a leader's commitment, we will be transformed.

Serve to Be Great

Jon Gordon

A team feels a leader's commitment when the leader takes the time to serve them. Jesus washed feet; Martin Luther King marched; Mother Teresa fed the poor and healed the sick. Over the years, I have met many leaders who serve their teams in simple, powerful ways. Many leaders think that as they gain power and responsibility, their teams should serve them more, but great leaders know that their job is to serve their teams. When you serve the team, you help them grow and they help you grow.

You can't serve yourself and your team at the same time. You have to decide whether you are going to serve *me* or *we*. You must decide if you are going to be a self-serving "leader" or a true leader who serves others. It's hard to be a servant-leader in today's world. Leaders are under more pressure than ever to perform. If you are a business leader you must answer to the stock market, the board, and shareholders. If you are a coach you must answer to your owner, general manager, and fan base. If you are a school leader you have to answer to your school board, superintendents, and parents of students. With expectations comes pressure and stress that drives a leader to survive, which leads to self-preservation rather than serving the team. When leaders become focused on the fruit instead of the root and worry about the outcome instead of the process of developing team members, they may survive in the short run, but they will not thrive in the long run. Self-serving leaders don't leave legacies that change the world for

Commitment

the better. They may win a few championships, make money, and achieve some fame in the short run, but true greatness is achieved when a leader brings out the greatness in others. Great leaders and coaches are great servants. A great coach sacrifices and serves in order to help team members become great. The big questions you must ask yourself each day are: What am I doing to serve my team and the people I lead? How can I serve them to help them be the best versions of themselves? How can I demonstrate my commitment to them? Remember, you don't have to be great to serve, but you have to serve to be great.

Commitment Starts at Home

Mike Smith

When I was fired as the head coach of the Atlanta Falcons, I had options to coach again. Ultimately, I chose not to coach this year because I know that commitment starts at home. I had been so committed to my football team over the years that it took me time to realize that my wife and daughter, who is in high school, need my commitment this year. It's been the best decision I've ever made. I've gone to almost all of my daughter's lacrosse games and even helped keep the stats book. Her coaches said I was the most detailed stat keeper they ever had. (Hey, when you are an NFL coach you learn how to focus on the details and stats.) I also spent more time helping my wife and I'm so thankful I did. I think as leaders and coaches we think that commitment, leadership, and service are about the big things but really they are about doing the little things to let your team know you are there for them.

Of course, I wish I was still coaching the Falcons because I believe strongly that we would have turned around the team. After all, Bill Cowher and the Pittsburgh Steelers had back-to-back losing seasons in his seventh and eighth years as head coach before righting the ship and winning a Super Bowl. I believe we could have done the same, but this experience has been a huge blessing that has helped me understand how important it is to commit at home. It's a lesson I want to share with all leaders and coaches out there. It doesn't matter how much success you have in your career; if you fail at home you are a failure. We only get one shot to be a parent and spouse, and we must give it everything we've got and commit to our "team" at home. When I return to coaching, I will be just as committed to the football team, but I will do a better job of committing to my home team. It's possible to do both. You just have to make both a priority.

Commitment Is Spelled T-I-M-E

Jon Gordon

Hearing Mike's story about committing at home reminds me of a few years ago, when I was thinking about my one word for the year. It was getting close to January 1 and I still didn't have my word. Finally it came to me while listening to the radio. My word was going to be "serve." I didn't choose the word; it chose me. I had been traveling a lot to speak to a number of companies, schools, and sports teams, and my wife and teenage children were struggling at home. I realized, like Mike, that I had to start serving at home. I had to show them I was committed to them. So I turned down a number of speaking engagements and made more *time* with my family. It turned out to be the hardest year of my life.

My daughter was not doing great in school. My wife and son were butting heads. My wife was stressed and having trouble managing it all. It was very frustrating because I wanted my kids to be self-starters like I was as a kid. I wanted my wife to be able to handle it all. Why did they need my help? Why couldn't I just focus on making a difference in the world? Why couldn't I have a different team? Yes, I admit it. I wanted a different team. Have you ever wanted a different team? If you are a leader, coach, or parent I know the answer is yes. Despite my frustration, I made the time to help my team get better. I drove my daughter to school each day and encouraged her. When she came home, I grilled her on her homework assignments and test topics to make sure she was preparing and studying. I put the kids to bed and prayed with them. I did the laundry often. I got very involved in their everyday challenges. In short, I became committed.

That December, my wife asked me what my word would be for the coming year. She asked if it was going to be "selfish" because she had never seen me do so much for my family. I told her no way. "Serve" was now a part of me and my commitment. Making the time to serve my family was how I showed I was truly committed to them. I realized that I didn't need a different team, but instead needed to become a better leader through my time and service. Everything in my being wanted to focus on ME but I was at my best when I focused on WE. I also realized a great truth for leaders. We have the team we have for a reason. The challenges we have with our team are meant to make us better leaders.

In the process of committing to my family and learning to serve, I became a better leader. Ironically, that's when my books and career took off. My son hurt his back playing tennis and my wife took him to the chiropractor, who asked how I was doing. My wife told him I was speaking at the World Leaders Conference with a bunch of famous people. The chiropractor said, "Well, Jon is famous." My son replied, "Not in our house. He does the laundry." When my wife told me this story I lit up. My son notices my commitment at home and that means everything. At the end of the day, I don't want to be a household name. I want to be a big name in my household. My daughter is doing great at school, my wife is much happier, and I'm helping my son become the best version of himself. I believe all success starts with making the team around you better.

When You Commit You Make Everyone Better

Mike Smith

When you talk about building a winning team and making the people around you better, you have to talk about Swen Nater. Swen was a community college All-American at Cypress College when John Wooden recruited him to play at UCLA. As the story goes, John told him that he wasn't going to play in a lot of games because they already had the best center in the world in Bill Walton, but Swen would have the opportunity to play against Bill Walton every day in practice. Wooden wanted the six-foot-eleven Nater to challenge and push Bill Walton to improve. Nater accepted his role during his time at UCLA and every day in practice he focused on one task: making

Bill Walton better. But while he was making Bill Walton better, something interesting happened. Swen also improved. Swen was the only player in ABA-NBA history to be drafted in the first round never having started a collegiate game. Swen was named the ABA rookie of the year and went on to have a 12-year career in the ABA-NBA. He is a great example of how, when you help your team get better, you get better. When you focus on helping others improve, you improve. Swen's commitment to his team helped him become a successful professional basketball player, and he's now an executive with Costco.

Speaking of making the people around you better, one of the most committed team members I've ever had the opportunity to coach was Roddy White. Most people only saw gameday Roddy White, but I was fortunate to see his commitment every day throughout the years. Roddy dealt with a number of injuries over the years, but he spent countless hours in the treatment room doing everything in his power to get healthy and back on the field. That is why Roddy was able to play in 133 consecutive games. The commitment he made to being healthy enough to play on Sundays was like none I have ever seen. There was no way that he was going to miss being out there with his teammates. His teammates saw his effort and commitment and it made them more committed as well.

Matt Ryan also showed his commitment by showing up on his off day to watch extra film. He didn't have to do it. He did it because he wanted to get better and be part of the process of putting the game plan together with the coaches. When we met with the team to install the plan, he would be a day ahead of the rest of the team. This commitment made the rest of the team better.

Tony Gonzales was not only committed to extra skill work but also to his nutrition. Tony was always looking for that edge that would allow him to outperform his opponents, and he knew that if he fueled his body with a properly balanced diet he was enhancing his chances to win on game day and enhancing his chances to be healthy throughout the season. This commitment rubbed off on other players on the team and more players were focused on fueling their bodies better.

Mike Peterson, who played for me in Jacksonville and joined us in Atlanta for his final three seasons, really showed how commitment makes a team better. Mike had been a starter his entire career and in 2012 he became a back-up player. That last season Mike's commitment to the team was at the highest level it had ever been. He did whatever he had to do to contribute to our success. He played on special teams, and he mentored the younger players.

When you have teammates like these who are committed, it will make everyone around them better. As a team member there are so many ways that you can contribute to the success of the team. It's not always about making the big play. It's about taking action and committing yourself to preparation, health, nutrition, practice, recovery, and all the ways that make you and the team better.

The Hard Hat

Jon Gordon

In my book *The Hard Hat*, I wrote about George Boiardi, who I believe was one of the greatest teammates to ever live. George played lacrosse at Cornell 11 years after I did. He died on the field in 2004.

The Cornell team carried a hard hat with them to every practice and game. It represented their blue-collar work ethic. Each year, a freshman who demonstrated the values of being a selfless, committed, hard-working teammate was selected to carry the hard hat. George was the carrier of the hard hat his freshman year, and after his death Cornell put his number, 21, on it so they could always remember his dedication and spirit. Over the years George and the hard hat came to define the Cornell lacrosse program and led to unprecedented success. George's coaches and teammates told me about his incredible commitment, and it's why 11 years after his death his influence on others continues to grow. He was the hardest worker and most selfless person on the team, and he served in a variety of ways. He made time for teammates who needed a ride home or to hear an encouraging word. He was the last to leave the locker room and always cleaned it up after his teammates left. He invited teammates in need of improvement to spend more time practicing with him in the off-season. He never wanted recognition, but simply to help his team get better. His teammates still evaluate themselves against the model George set, and they wonder if they are living committed lives and serving their current team members enough. Today, people who have never even met George have raised their commitment to a greater level because of his example. It's amazing the impact one committed leader who serves his team can have on the lives of others. If this resonates with you, then decide to put on your hard hat and get to work.

It's Not about You

Jon Gordon

I first met Carl Liebert when he was the CEO of 24 Hour Fitness and invited me to speak to the leaders of his company. Carl was a graduate of the Naval Academy and played on the Navy basketball team with David Robinson. After a long and successful career with Home Depot, Carl brought his servant-leadership approach to 24 Hour Fitness. Before he became CEO, the executives of 24 Hour Fitness had personal trainers visit their homes to train them in private, but Carl made it mandatory for the executives to train at the centers so they could spend more time interacting with staff members and identify better ways to serve their team and customers. He also required executives to work for a week in one of their locations each year. Some executives chose to work in membership sales while others worked as physical trainers or in membership services. The experience helped the 24 Hour Fitness leaders to not only better serve their teams but also to understand the needs of their members. It demonstrated their commitment to everyone, and it made all the difference.

After successfully transforming 24 Hour Fitness, Carl joined the team at USAA, where he continues to demonstrate his servant leadership and commitment as the Chief Operating Officer. I have spent time at USAA and have personally witnessed the way he leads with authenticity, humility, and commitment. He asks for input and invites feedback. He shares his one word with everyone in the company and invites everyone to share their words with him. He looks for ways to develop the strengths of each team member and coaches them to be the best versions of themselves. Most of all, he leads with humility, knowing it's not about him—it's about his team. He would be mortified that I'm writing about him because he doesn't seek recognition, but I had to tell you about him because his example is so powerful. Remember, it's not about you. It's about committing yourself to your team.

Lose Your Ego

Mike Smith

To be a humble leader like Swen, George, and Carl, you must lose your ego. I believe to be a successful leader you have to have an ego that drives you to be great, *but* you must give up your ego and serve your team in order to be great. You must lose your ego so you can stop focusing on yourself and start focusing on your team. After all, humility doesn't mean you think less of yourself. It just means you think of yourself less and your team more (to paraphrase C.S. Lewis).

Too many leaders worry about what the media says about them. They worry about what successes and failures look like to the world outside the locker room. Unfortunately we've seen too many business leaders and coaches make decisions based on their egos rather than their teams. Sometimes when teams lose, instead of taking the blame, coaches blame the players. Once coaches do this, they lose in the locker room. We've seen coaches lock their players out of the locker room and then tell the media it was because they didn't play hard. Well, if they didn't play hard, whose fault is that? If the coach didn't inspire them to play hard by creating the right culture, then the coach needs to take the blame, not pin it on the team. Instead of locking the players out of the locker room, the coach should say, "I'm locking myself out of the locker room because I didn't do a good enough job leading my team this week."

Similarly, we've seen sales managers blame their salespeople for not hitting their numbers. Again, if people are not hitting their numbers then managers need to work with them to help them get there. If underperformers aren't willing to work and contribute to the team, then they need to find a different team. Coach them to improve or let them off the team, but don't blame them for your lack of success. We see politicians blame everyone except themselves for the country's problems. We need leaders now more than ever who care more about helping others and solving problems than what people think of them.

Our rule of thumb is that you have to care more about what your team thinks about you than what the forces outside the locker room think of you. Whether you are a business leader, school leader, or non-profit leader, never throw your team under the bus. Don't try to make them look bad so you can look good. Instead, own your weaknesses then improve. Lose your ego and let your team and the world know you have their back. Then get back to work and make sure you are doing your part and they are doing their parts to get better. When you lose your ego, you will win the hearts and minds of your team—then you will win in the locker room.

As a leader of the team or organization, you are going to be put in many situations in which you need to choose whether you are going to take the fall or pin the blame on someone else. The only option for leaders who serve their teams is to take responsibility for everything that happens on the field or in the marketplace. No matter what occurs, never put blame on your players or coaches. If a player blows a coverage or runs the wrong route, you take responsibility because you should have done a better job of preparing them to execute their roles. Take responsibility instead of blaming others in the hope that it will deflect the criticism away from you. Remember, as the leader of the team or organization, the buck stops with you.

When something goes wrong on the field, do everything in your power to make sure that no one individual player or coach is going to take the blame. The responsibility lands squarely on the shoulders of the head coach, who is also accountable for getting it fixed. Deal with the situation and those involved in a private setting and figure out why it happened and what everyone can do differently in the future to make sure that it does not happen again.

There have been many times after a game or during the week when I have been asked about a specific play on offense or defense that was not successful. I knew the media wanted me to point the finger at someone specific, but I wouldn't do it. For example, in a game against Tampa Bay, we gave up a long touchdown pass in the second quarter. The closest player to the receiver was our safety and everyone who did not know the defensive huddle call assumed he was at fault and gave up the touchdown pass. The coverage that was called actually had the cornerback responsible for the deep zone and the safety covering another area of the field. The safety almost made a spectacular play on the ball by breaking on it while it was in the air. While everyone assumed that he was the culprit, he was actually close to doing something extraordinary. When asked about the play I said, "I have to do a better job of making sure that we are all on the same page in regards to what is being called in the huddle." I went on to tell the questioner that he should not make assumptions as to who is at fault without knowing what the coverage call was in the huddle.

The team will function more effectively when it has leaders and team members who refuse to blame their teammates. Matt Ryan is a great model of a servant-leader who understands the need to protect his teammates and take responsibility instead of assigning blame towards anyone else. Even when a receiver ran the wrong route and the pass was intercepted, Matt would take responsibility for the miscue even though he was not responsible. His team knew he had their backs and as a result would run and play harder for him.

Of course, there's a time and place to address how we are going to correct the miscue—that is what coaching and leading is all about—but that is not a public setting and it should be done with as much positive reinforcement as possible. As the great NBA coach Chuck Daly would say, shout praise in public and whisper criticism in private.

Commitment Requires Sacrifice

Jon Gordon

The ultimate commitment is sacrifice. To build a great team, your team has to know and feel that you would run into a burning building to save them. They have to know that you are willing to sacrifice yourself for their gain. Great leaders ignore the easy road and build their teams by taking the more difficult path, one that is filled with service and sacrifice. This requires you to lose your ego and love your team. If you love someone you are willing to sacrifice for them. If you love your team you will do whatever it takes to build them up, even if it means tearing yourself down.

This is precisely the reason why I love Mike and the way he leads. This is why I decided to write this book with him. I know the man he is. I know his character and integrity and the sacrifices he has made. When he was fired by the Atlanta Falcons, he took the blame even though he wasn't the only one at fault. I didn't see or hear anyone else in the organization accept blame for their losing seasons the last two years. I didn't hear any leaders from the organization step up and say, "You know, we got away from our culture and process. We should have done a better job drafting pass rushers." Nope. They simply fired the coach and let him take the blame.

Mike Smith stood there alone at the podium in front of millions of people and said, "I'm the coach, and wins and losses are my responsibility. It's my fault." He didn't blame his general manager. He didn't blame his players. He didn't blame his coaching staff. He didn't blame anyone. He did what he had done for his entire coaching career, including his seven years with the Falcons. He put his team and organization first and sacrificed for them. The media and fans may point fingers, but those who played for him and know him know that he always gave his all to them—and he always will. He's a committed leader who will always sacrifice for his team.

Chapter 7

Care

Relationships are the foundation upon which winning teams are built, and all great relationships are based on value, respect, love, trust, and care.

Caring Is a Strategy

Jon Gordon

 In Water Isaacson's biography of Steve Jobs, he shared a story about Steve helping his father build a fence when he was a young boy. His father told him he must care about crafting the back of the fence as much as the front. When Steve asked why the back mattered when no one would see how it was crafted, his father said, "But you will know." Steve's father taught him to care more, and years later he went on to create Apple products with such care that they generated feelings of awe, loyalty, and passion among the brand's millions of new customers. It wasn't an accident. Jonathan Ive, the man who designed many iconic Apple products, said, "We believe our customers can sense the care we put into our products." Apple cared about the work they were doing and the products they were creating, and in turn their customers cared about them.

I believe caring is one of the greatest success strategies of all. The greatest organizations on the planet care about the work they do, the products they create, and the services they provide. I've been fortunate to work with many of the most successful companies in the world, and I have discovered they all have a unique way that shows they care—I call it a "caring trademark"—and this causes them to stand out from their competition. Apple designs products that are so simple to use my 74-year-old father can do so without a hitch. Online retailer Zappos provides free shipping and returns. USAA will go to superhuman lengths to assist its members with their financial security. Publix supermarket employees walk people to the correct spot on the shelf when a customer can't find a product. Les Schwab Tire Centers require their staff to run outside and greet their customers when they get out of the car. Chick-fil-A employees say "My pleasure" instead of "No problem." Fitz at Rosenblum's clothiers in Jacksonville did something to show me he cared and I'll never forget it. I bought a suit from him a few years ago and decided to wear it for the first time. Not only did it fit and feel great, but right before I got on stage to speak, I found a card from Fitz in the jacket pocket. It said, "I hope you are doing something positive right now." It's no surprise that Fitz and Rosenblum's have such a loyal following and a thriving business.

A few years ago a carpenter came to my house to do some work. When I asked him how business had been the last few years, during the recession, he responded, "I've been busier than ever." It made perfect sense. He's considered the best in our city. He is known for the care he puts into his work and has a reputation for caring about his customers. He stands out from the competition and is in more demand than ever. When you care you stand out in a world where so many seem like they don't care.

Care More

Jon Gordon

When I spoke to the Pittsburgh Pirates last year I asked the players, "Who here believes they can work harder than they currently do?" Every guy on the team raised his hand and every person on every team I have asked since, also raise their hands. The next question naturally is, "If you know you can work harder, then why don't you?" The answer: to work harder you have to care more. When you care more, you give a little more time, a little more effort, a little more energy, and a little more love to the things and people you care about. You may be a good team, but to be a great team you have to care more. Care about the work you do and how it contributes to the team. Care about the people you work with. Care about the mission of your team. Care more about the people you lead. Those who care build great things that others care about.

Speaking of the Pittsburgh Pirates, they are a great example of an organization that cares more. We can measure revenue, costs, wins, and losses but it's hard to measure and quantify caring. Even so, when we experience an organization that cares, we can tell there is something very different about them. We feel it when we walk around the building, store, offices, or locker room. We see it in the messages on the walls. We hear it when we talk to the leaders and observe the people of the organization. People who are part of a team that cares think, act, lead, and serve differently.

When I visited the Pittsburgh Pirates for the first time, at their pre-season training camp in 2013, they had just won 94 games and made it to the post-season. It was the first time they had a winning record since 1992 and I'm convinced their culture of caring is a big reason why. As I walked around, I noticed the "Pirates' Creed" posted throughout their facilities, conveying the characteristics, beliefs, values, and cultural expectations of how each person in the organization should think, act, and approach their work as a member of the Pirates.

When I spoke to Kyle Stark, the assistant general manager, he told me that their bigger purpose as an organization is to change the world of baseball by turning boys into men and developing players into professionals on and off the field. He said, "Our goal is to be the most cohesive team in the world and our mindset is to focus on the process of getting better every day." There was no talk of home runs, wins, or losses—just purpose, process, and teamwork.

The Pirates, like Southwest Airlines, Northwestern Mutual, and many great companies have discovered that it's not the numbers that motivate people. It's the culture, caring, and purpose that drive the numbers. If you want to win, you don't focus on winning. You focus on the culture, people, and process that produce wins. Kyle and the Pirates also know that it doesn't matter what signs and messages you have posted on the walls if your leaders and managers don't model it and your team doesn't live and breathe it. You must have leaders who care more about everyone else and everything they do.

The Pirates conduct a daily leadership meeting during spring training where leadership coach Rod Olson shares a daily tip with all the coaches in the organization (minor and major leagues). They also bring in a bunch of outside speakers like me to develop their leaders and reinforce their values knowing culture, caring, and leadership go hand in hand.

When I met and talked with Clint Hurdle, the 2013 Manager of the Year for the Pirates, I knew why the culture had come alive in the hearts and minds of his players. Clint is a big man with a bigger servant's heart. A former MLB player, he knows what it takes to be a winner but more importantly his players know that he loves them. He wants to win but he's more interested in helping his players become winners. I've found that a leader who cares builds a team that cares. Then together they care about their effort. They care about getting better. They care about each other. They care about the organization. They care about their culture. They care more so they do more. The culture may have been designed in the office but Clint's presence, coaching, and caring make it come to life in the clubhouse and on the field. I can't predict how well the Pirates will do this year. Injuries happen and in sports sometimes things don't go your way, but after experiencing their caring culture, I can predict that everyone in the Pirates organization will do everything they can to strive for greatness, and more often than not, this will lead to a great outcome.

Create a Culture of Caring

Jon Gordon

To build a winning team it's essential to build a culture of caring. To build a culture of caring you must be a leader who cares. When you care, you will inspire others to care. Find ways to extend yourself to others and serve them. Write a note. Make a call. Go out of your way to serve someone. Go beyond the expected. People know you care when you go out of your way to show them they matter. A smile, an encouraging word, an extra five minutes of time, solving a problem, listening to an employee, sacrificing for a friend, and helping a team member through a challenging time can make all the difference. Never underestimate the importance of making time to make someone feel special. Then, when you develop a reputation for caring and others expect more from you, you continue to deliver more than they expect. With each caring act you are saying, "I am here to love you and serve you," and when this happens, you attract more love and success. Your team will love working with you. People will tell stories at parties and gatherings about you. Authors may even write books about you. Caring is the ultimate team-building strategy. People make it complicated but it's simple:

1. Care about the work you do.
2. Surround yourself with people who care.
3. Show your team you care about them.
4. Build a team that cares about one another.
5. Together show your customers/fans/students/patients that you care about them.

When we make caring a strategy and create a culture of caring, we stand out and create success that lasts.

Show You Care

Mike Smith

I couldn't agree more with Jon. If you want to build a winning team, you must show that you care. It sounds obvious and simple but too often we forget to show we care. We get busy, stressed, self-consumed, and don't take the time to let others know we care about them. When you care about someone, you show them that they matter and make them feel important. You show your team that you care by being present when you are with them. You don't look around them or over them. You look right at them and let them know they have your full attention. You take sincere interest in their professional work and personal lives. Having one-on-one personal contact is the most effective way to show people that you care. When you are the leader it is impossible to have these interactions daily, but over time these encounters add up and this lets your team know that you care. When you care about your team they will give their all to you.

I think the best indicator that people care is not what they say about themselves, but what others say about them. Do others say you care? Can they identify ways that you care? Jon told me that he asked a number of my players how I showed that I cared and they said that I listened and visited them in the treatment room, and made time for them and cared about them as people, not just football players. They said they knew I had their backs and did everything in my power to help them be the best they could be. I don't think I'm perfect and I certainly don't like to talk about my accomplishments, but one of the things I'm most proud of, beyond wins and losses, is that my team knows that I cared about them. I believe that, at the end of the day, what matters most is that we made an impact in the lives of others. As a coach it's a great opportunity and responsibility, and it is the coaches who cared about me who I remember most.

I have been very fortunate to have had coaches, friends, and family members who have really cared about me. These people have taken a special interest and have provided me with a wealth of knowledge from their experiences. It is these experiences that have molded me into the coach and person that I am. I know for a fact I would have never been a coach in the NFL if it wasn't for these people.

My high school coach, Phil Richart, was one of the many mentors who taught me about the importance of being a caring leader and person. During my senior year at Father Lopez High School, I was injured in the second game of the season. The injury ended my high-school career and diminished my opportunities to play football in college. Needless to say, I was crushed. The high school that I attended had a small staff of six coaches, two of whom were volunteers. I always had an interest in coaching, even at an early age. My father was a junior-high coach and I grew up hanging around practices, starting at the age of five. Coach Richart allowed me to take part in some of the coaching duties involving meetings with the linebackers. He took me on scouting trips to watch upcoming opponents. He allowed me to work on the field with the players. He showed me that he cared about me beyond what I could contribute on the field. He got me my first hands-on experiences in coaching and showed me how to be a caring leader.

Until he passed away in August of 2013, he would send me a text with his critique and words of wisdom and encouragement after every game that I coached with the Atlanta Falcons. I always looked forward to his message because it showed that he still cared. Coach Richart was just one of many people who showed me how caring impacts others. Speaking of texts and caring, my mom is a great woman who cared and taught me to care greatly. During a game against the New Orleans Saints, we were leading in the fourth quarter. The Saints had moved the ball for a couple of first downs and the momentum was starting to shift their way with just under two minutes to play. Our right cornerback, Brent Grimes, made a spectacular play and intercepted Drew Brees's pass inside of our 15-yard line. It was a game-ending play because we were going to be able to run the clock out by snapping the ball and taking a knee. When Brent made the play, of course, our sideline and the fans in the Georgia Dome went crazy. As the play was ending I saw a penalty flag thrown by the back judge flying through the air. He called us for defensive pass interference. I absolutely lost it, and in an instant the Motorola headset that I was wearing was on the turf, where it busted into about five pieces. With the help of our equipment manager, I tried to pick them up and put them back together while the assistant equipment manager tried to give me a back-up headset. It was a little hectic there for about 30 seconds. I am sure it was quite a sight for those who were focusing on me, the coach, throwing a tantrum. We finally got the mess on the sideline cleaned up and went on to hold the Saints out of the end zone and win the game.

After the game I talked to the team and had my regular postgame wrap up meeting with our vice president of communications, Reggie Roberts, before going to the press conference. The message light on my cell phone started to flash. I picked up the device and saw that it was a text from my mother. I don't think I had ever received a text from my mom prior to that day. When I opened it up, it started, "KENNETH MICHAEL"—and let me tell you, when my mother calls me by my first and middle name, I know what is about to hit the fan. She went on: "YOUR FATHER AND I DID NOT RAISE YOU TO ACT LIKE THAT IN FRONT OF HUNDREDS OF THOUSANDS OF PEOPLE. THAT WAS NOT A VERY GOOD EXAMPLE THAT YOU SET FOR YOUR DAUGHTER, SEVEN BROTHERS AND SISTERS, AND ELEVEN NIECES AND NEPHEWS." I think you probably get the gist of her message. Needless to say, my mom will always be my mom. It does not matter how old I am. This was one time I wished the cell phone had never been invented, but she cared, and I love her for that.

More than a Uniform and Number

Mike Smith

If you want to build a winning team, you must value all team members for who they are, not just what they do. You have to see them as more than uniforms and numbers. You can't look at your team as X's and O's on a whiteboard or costs on a financial spreadsheet. Whether they are being paid as professional athletes, receiving scholarships for playing a college sport, employees in your company, or people who can help you win a high-school championship, you have to remind yourself that under each uniform or business suit is a person who has challenges, personal issues, pain, hurt, and human wants and needs. Every person, no matter how successful, wants to be appreciated, respected, and valued. Everyone wants to feel cared about. Everyone, ultimately, wants to be loved.

Good coaches know X's and O's, but great coaches also know their players. It's your job as a leader to know and love your team members. Even with all the pressure to win and succeed, always remember that it's through relationships and human connections that this happens. Get to know your team and see them as more than numbers, and they will see you as more than a number. They will be loyal to you and work harder for you. They will want to work with you because you care about them. Relationships are the foundation upon which winning teams are built, and all great relationships are based on value, respect, love, trust, and care.

Transactional versus Transformational

Mike Smith

One of the most important decisions you must make as a leader is whether you will be transactional or transformational. Joe Ehrmann is a former NFL player with the Baltimore Colts who I had the opportunity to hear speak when I was an assistant for the Ravens. He is also the author of *InSideOut Coaching*, which eloquently distinguishes between transactional and transformational leaders. On the one hand, transactional coaches see their teams as a bunch of numbers who are meant to help them succeed and win. They focus on how everyone can help them find success and improve their coaching careers in order to rise up the ladder. Their teams exist to serve their career growth and pump up their egos. Transformational coaches, on the other hand, see their role as a transformer of lives who helps each team member become the best version of him or herself. Transformational leaders believe their job is to serve their team members in order to help them grow in skill and character. Transformational coaches still want to win, but they know their foremost job is to develop people, serve their teams, and transform lives. Ironically, when transformational leaders focus on these things, they often end up winning a lot. Transactional coaches may win in the short run, but their approach is not sustainable. Transformational coaches invest in the root and, over time, it produces a lot of fruit.

Love Tough

Jon Gordon

I also read Joe Ehrmann's book, *InSideOut Coaching*, and it was transformative for me as a parent, leader, and person. I realized that as an athlete I had received a lot of my recognition and praise by performing and winning. My identity was tied up in my performance. As a parent, I was doing the same to my children. Their performance was all about how it made me look and feel, not about how playing a sport helped them develop as people. I changed and became a transformational parent and everything changed for the better. Being a caring, transformational leader, however, doesn't mean that you are weak and don't challenge the people you lead. Because you care, you challenge them to be their best. Because you love them, you don't allow them to settle for less. Because you expect more, you challenge them to do more.

I believe in tough love, but love must come first. If your team knows that you care about them, they will allow you to push and challenge them to be their best. The great leaders I have worked with over the years practice love tough, not tough love. They invest so much in their team members that they earn the right to challenge them and help them accomplish more than they ever thought possible. When you care, you will take the time to invest in relationships with your team members, and through those relationships you will both encourage and challenge them to grow into the best versions of themselves.

Discover Your Caring Trademark

Jon Gordon

I mentioned earlier that caring is a strategy, and the most successful companies have a unique way to show they care, something I call a *caring trademark*. I believe great leaders who build winning teams have a caring trademark as well. If you've followed Derek Jeter's career and watched his improbable game-winning hit in his final at bat in Yankee Stadium, you know that Derek treated every at bat like it was his last and that's what made his last at bat so special. No one worked harder, played with more passion, or cared more about honoring the game of baseball. His hustle, passion, commitment, and work ethic have become his caring trademark over the last 20 years.

While Jeter always sprinted to first base and treated every at bat as a sacred experience, Doug Conant's caring trademark was writing over 10,000 thank-you notes to employees while he was the CEO of Campbell Soup. Rita Pierson, a life-changing educator, had a caring trademark in how she encouraged and believed in her students. She talked about this in a TED talk, which is still one of my favorite all-time speeches. Even though she passed away, her legacy and caring trademark live on in the students she taught. Business services firm Gallagher

Bassett is helmed by CEO Scott Hudson, whose caring trademark is a weekly personal newsletter highlighting what he cares about in work and life sent to the more than 5,000 global employees. Interestingly, his employees often write back to him with personal stories of their own, further promoting a culture of open communication and caring. Drew Watkins, the superintendent of Prosper ISD, writes a personal note to every graduating senior. This past year when I asked teachers how he gets information to know what to write, they said he knows them each personally. He doesn't have some super-human memory. He just cares and gets to know his students. Dabo Swinney's caring trademark is the belief he instills in his players—he believes in them so much that they believe in themselves. Cori Close, the UCLA women's basketball coach, once had a player who was sick in the hospital. Cori stayed with her the entire time. She wouldn't leave. Her caring trademark is that she treats her players like family. The same goes for Sherri Coale, the University of Oklahoma women's basketball coach, and Rhonda Revelle, the University of Nebraska softball coach. They invest as much of their time and energy developing their players' character and mindset as they do in athletic skill.

When it comes to caring trademarks the list is endless. Someone could write a book about all the unique ways that great organizations and leaders show they care, but even if a book were written, I wouldn't want you to copy someone else. The key is to create your own caring trademark to fit you.

So think about who you are and what you stand for. Identify ways you love to show you care. Decide how you want to make a difference. What do you want to be known for? Your caring trademark should express who you are, demonstrate your values in action, and reflect your mission to make a difference and serve others. When you show you care in your own unique style, you will be well on your way to building a winning team.

When You Care, Your Team Will Care

Mike Smith

One of the great benefits of caring, besides developing great relationships with your team, is that it is contagious. When you care, your team will care. I saw this firsthand during my time with the Falcons. No matter what our record was, our team cared about our effort, performance, and winning. Whether we were an 8-4 team or a 4-8 team, the effort was always the same and we never stopped competing. While the media may not have noticed, and many who focused on only our win-loss record could have cared less about our effort, I cared that our team cared. I knew it meant that we hadn't lost in the locker room. You see, winning in the locker room doesn't always guarantee you'll win on the field or the court. Many other things have to work out for you. Sometimes things just don't work out and the ball does not bounce your way. Sometimes you experience a strange season, as every coach will attest, but I have found that caring and winning in the locker room will greatly increase your probability of winning on the scoreboard. When you care, you will build a team that cares and plays hard regardless of their record. Over time, this creates consistency of effort, which creates long-term success.

The Big C

It's not one of the 7 C's because it's in a class all by itself. It's the C that brings all the other C's together and transforms principles and ideas into action and ultimately a winning team. It all comes down to the Big C: coaching.

Today there's a lot of talk about leadership in sports, business, health care, and education; however, the concept of coaching is often ignored. It shouldn't be. It's an essential part of a leader's role. Now more than ever, leaders must coach the teams they lead to help them grow and become better leaders. True leaders don't create followers. They create more leaders. And this is accomplished through great coaching. Whether it's the executive leadership team of a Fortune 500 company, a sports team, an emergency room team, military team, or a school team you must coach the people you lead to develop, mentor, encourage, and guide them. This not only improves them, it improves you and your relationships, connections, and organization.

By coaching up and coaching down you create your culture. By coaching with optimism and positivity you become contagious. By coaching your team and mentoring them individually you earn their trust and connect with them. By being consistent, their trust in you is strengthened. By helping them get better through adversity and challenges you show you are committed to their growth and progress. By caring about them, you give everything you have to help your team become all they are meant to be.

We want to encourage you so that regardless of your position or role within your organization, you coach others to be their best. If you are the principal of a school, make the time to coach your teachers. Research shows that principals who coach their teachers to be better instructors create greater student performance. If you are a leader of a company, invest time to coach your leadership team and encourage them to coach the people who report to them. We've seen CEOs coach their leadership teams to be better leaders, which led to improved relationships, engagement, and performance throughout the organization. If you are a manager, coach the people you manage. Ask them to identify their vision and goals, and then ask how you can help them achieve them. Help them become the best versions of themselves and they will help the company grow. If you are in business, ask your frontline customer service employees to coach your customers. When you coach and guide your customers, they will become your customers for life.

A lot of coaches in the sports world read business and leadership books. But we believe that business, education, and non-profit leaders can learn a lot about coaching from the sports world. Billy Graham said one coach will impact more people in a year than most people do in a lifetime. If you doubt this, do an informal survey and ask people who made a difference in their lives. Teachers and coaches are up there with family members. Yet, we don't often hear people say, "My manager changed my life" or "My CEO changed my life" or "My hospital administrator changed my life." It doesn't have to be this way. If you decide to invest in others and coach them the way great coaches do in sports, you can have an incredible impact. Great coaches succeed not because they are great, but because they bring out the greatness in others. You can utilize the 7 C's to become a Big C and start coaching today.

The Other Big C

We almost didn't include this C in the book because we naturally assumed that everyone knows how important character is to build a great team. After all, you can be the greatest coach on the planet, but if your team lacks character you will fail to reach your potential. Yet, given how many coaches and leaders attempt to build a team by focusing on talent instead of character, we had to talk about it. It's the other Big C because without *Character* you can't coach a team to be successful, you can't build a great culture, and the other C's don't work very well.

We see it all the time in sports and business. A talented individual with character flaws makes a bad decision that affects the entire team and organization. That's why when building a team you want to build it with both talent and character. Don't just settle for talent. Talent without character is like a race car with no steering wheel. It looks great from the outside and drives fast, but without something guiding it, a crash is very likely. Talent isn't enough. Talent doesn't last. It will only take you so far. Talent without character is also like an expensive car with no gas. It's useless without the fuel that drives it. Character drives talent toward greatness. If you have people who are humble, hungry, hard working, honest, dedicated, selfless, loyal, passionate, and accountable they will be the kind of people who develop their talent and make the right decisions to benefit themselves and the team. Character guides and drives your team members to be their best and bring out the best in others.

John Wooden and Mike Krzyzewski (Coach K) are two great examples of coaches who built their teams with talent and "high character" people, and they have succeeded over the long haul because of this winning approach. They knew that high character student athletes were the foundational pieces in building a winning team and culture, and that communication, connection, commitment, and caring were the cement that bonded the pieces together. They knew the character necessary to build their culture and in turn they created a culture that built and developed that character. This is an important point because while they only recruited players with both talent and character, they were also leaders who developed the character of their players. They didn't see each person as a finished product. They saw their role as a developer of character as well as talent.

If you were wondering what to do with a team that may currently have some low character people on it, then you can take a page from Coach Wooden and Coach K and make it a priority to develop their characters. If you are a high school coach reading this, we understand that you don't have the luxury of recruiting only high character guys and girls on your team. But you have a great opportunity to develop their characters and have a huge impact on their life. You can develop their characters so they are the kind of people that a Coach K would want to recruit. We believe in giving every person a chance to become a high character person. Do everything you can to develop character. Make it a part of your curriculum! Utilize the Big C to develop the other Big C. Coach to develop Character. But remember and heed this warning: if you have someone who isn't willing to improve, and he's making decisions detrimental to himself and the team, then you will have no choice but to let him off the team. If someone is going to crash, don't let him hurt the rest of the team. But do everything you can to prevent the crash in the first place. And just because you let them off the team doesn't mean you can't continue to help them. You can still try to help them become the best versions of themselves. Character doesn't just build great teams. More importantly, it builds great people.

THE MODEL

The 7 C's to Build a Winning Team and the 2 Big C's that Drive the Process

Beyond the 7 C's

There's more to building a winning team than just the 7 C's. Other principles are just as important and, while they don't begin with the letter C, we would be remiss if we didn't share them. In this spirit, here are some of our key areas of focus and things to consider as you build your team.

Integrity

Jon Gordon

In 2014 I attended the Cornell Hall of Fame induction dinner, where I heard David Eckel, a cross country track and field champion, share a story from the fall of 1955 during the Heptagonal Championship in Van Cortlandt Park in New York City. David said he had led most of the race with his Cornell teammate, Michael Midler, right behind him in second place and Doug Brew from Dartmouth about 60 yards behind them. With about a mile left in the race, David and Michael took a wrong turn and headed down a path away from the finish line. Doug saw them going the wrong way and shouted to them, "You are off course! You are off course! You are going the wrong way!" David and Michael quickly got back on the right path and finished in first and second place while Doug Brew finished third. That year, Cornell won the individual and team championship, and if it wasn't for Doug's integrity, it never would have happened. David and Doug still keep in touch and Doug said he never regretted it. He felt it was the right thing to do and that the Cornell guys would have done the same thing for him. David told me that he spoke about Doug because he knew his induction to the Hall of Fame might not have happened if it wasn't for the integrity and help of his competitor.

Doug Brew could have easily let his competition go the wrong way and become a champion. Instead he became a champion of integrity. Sixty years later, people are still sharing this story and talking about it. When you lead with integrity you won't always win, but you will always do the right thing. When leading your team, you have to ask yourself, "Am I building this team for the short run or long run? Do I want immediate gratification or sustained success? Will I lead with integrity or violate my principles and compromise my ethics?" There's a lot of temptation to make decisions that lead to worldly success but unfortunately, when you do this, you will lose your soul in the process. You may win today but you will lose in the end. Always remember that there's tremendous power generated from leading with integrity. It may not be manifested this year or next, but over time this power will lead to powerful results. There's only one way to build a winning team and that's the right way. Stay the course. Lead with integrity. Do the right thing. You'll be glad you did.

Be Passionate, Not Emotional

Mike Smith

It is important to understand that there is a difference between passion and emotion. The difference between the two is that passion involves a *belief* about something. Emotions involve *feelings* about something. You want to be a passionate leader who makes decisions that are based on belief and principle over those that are based on feeling. After all, you won't always feel like doing the right thing, but if you live based on belief and principle you will do what needs to be done. Sometimes you don't feel like working hard, but your belief in improvement and growth moves you to do it. When you have a belief in something, there is a process that you have gone through to form that belief. When you are passionate about a subject, you are well versed in it and the decisions that you make are going to be well thought out and studied. Emotion, on the other hand, causes you to act in illogical ways more often than not. An emotional decision is usually a spur-of-the-moment, by–the-seat–of-your-pants decision that has not been well thought out and often leads to poor outcomes. Emotions are hard to control and they are usually self-serving and illogical, weakening your leadership. Passion, on the other hand, is the engine that drives you to be a great leader and build a winning team.

Create Your Own Style of Leadership

Mike Smith

How many times in sports have we seen the hot assistant coach from a highly successful program get hired by another team and fail miserably? It happens quite often in sports and business. The reason for failure is that new leaders come into a team or organization and attempt to mimic the leadership style of the head coach or CEO from their previous jobs instead of being the person they truly are. They believe that if they do it exactly the same way, they will have the same amount of success. We have seen time after time that it is a recipe for disaster. It is difficult to be a genuine leader if you are making decisions for your team or organization solely because that is the way the previous team did it, or that's how someone else did it. Leadership doesn't work like this. No two teams or organizations are the same. Each will have a different leadership structure and organizational culture that you will have to deal with. You must be the person who you have always been and use all of the experiences that you have had throughout your career to mold and create your own style of leadership. What worked for one leader and coach may not work for you. One person might have the kind of personality that is tough but likeable, and another might be tough but not likeable at all. Some people might be able to lead a certain way because of the experiences they have had, the success they have earned, and the respect they have garnered. If you try to lead like them without having gone through the same experiences, it won't work for you.

When I became the head coach of the Atlanta Falcons I borrowed ideas, routines, and principles from the great leaders I worked with and admired but created a framework and approach that fit my leadership style and personality. I took all the experiences and lessons I've learned over the years and made them my own. You have to be yourself.

Everyone else is taken. Create your own style that fits who you are and you will have a much greater chance of building a winning team.

Leadership Is Both Macro and Micro

Jon Gordon

Macro-leadership involves culture, vision, strategy, and the ability to lead at the organizational level, while micro-leadership involves leading at the team and individual levels. Macro- and micro-leadership require a different set of skills. While visiting West Point I learned that when cadets graduate, most are technically better at macro-leadership than micro-leadership. Like many leaders and managers in the civilian world, they have to learn to coach, lead, and build their teams at the micro level. When thinking about your own leadership, it's helpful to think about leading at both the macro and micro levels. Today more than ever micro-leadership is essential to build winning teams and organizations.

Lead Your Leaders

Jon Gordon

I realize that not everyone reading this book is a head coach, CEO, or main boss. Many of us are in positions where we help lead a team but we are not at the top of the organizational chart. I can relate—even at home I'm second in command. But I've learned that no matter what role you play in your organization, you can lead from where you are and help your leaders be their best. For example, upon graduating from West Point, a cadet will commission as an officer and be placed to lead a platoon. West Point cadets are encouraged to listen to the advice of their non-commissioned officer (NCO), who is often an expert at micro-leadership (coaching). I had an officer tell me that when he arrived to lead his platoon, his NCO coached him and gave him leadership advice behind the scenes that made all the difference with his platoon. I greatly admire the NCOs who do not possess the title of a commissioned officer but who coach and serve their leaders in a powerful way. A big part of leadership is leading from where you are and influencing people around you regardless of your title, rank, or position.

My friend Brendan Suhr was the assistant coach to Chuck Daly for the Detroit Pistons NBA Championship team and the original U.S. Olympic Dream Team. Brendan wasn't considered the leader but he coached up the leader and down to the team. Because of him, both the leader and the team were successful. Anyone who knows Brendan knows he has spent a lifetime in the role of leading the leader. His title is assistant coach but his leadership and influence are of primary importance. Brendan told me that a suggestion, a question, a story, a book recommendation, and advice behind the scenes can make all the difference. Even to this day Brendan is a coach of coaches, leading Coaching U. Live and helping leaders get better. He believes that, with help, stronger leaders will build better teams. If you want to build a winning team, this means that there may be times when you have to lead your leader and build him or her up.

Focus on the Process

Jon Gordon

When people ask me how long it takes to become an overnight success, I say at least 10 years. There's no such thing as an overnight success. Success takes time. Building a winning team and organization requires grit and perseverance. Consider that Starbucks did not reach store number five until 13 years into its history. Sam Walton did not open his second store until 7 years after starting his company. Dr. Seuss wanted to burn the manuscript of his first book after it was rejected by 27 publishers (thankfully, he didn't). And it took John Wooden almost two decades to win his first championship at UCLA. In the weekly newsletter of the John R. Wooden Course (woodencourse.com), "Wooden's Wisdom," Craig Impelman wrote:

> *March 15, 1963; Provo, Utah: Arizona State defeats UCLA 93-79 in the first game of the NCAA Western Regional Tournament . . . and the final score made the game sound closer than it was. Arizona State was leading 62-31 at halftime. That season was Coach Wooden's 17th at UCLA; that appearance was his fifth NCAA tournament. And in those tournament games, he had a painful record of only three wins and nine losses. But something was different about this particular game. Coach Wooden had just added a new dimension to his defense: a full-court 2-2-1 zone press that was designed to force teams to shoot the ball quickly. It had worked to perfection in the Arizona State game; the Sun Devils were forced over and over again to shoot the ball quickly. Unfortunately for UCLA, they couldn't miss a shot. But Coach Wooden liked what he saw.*

The final score did not discourage Coach or cause him to panic because of his philosophy: "Success is peace of mind which is a direct result of self-satisfaction in knowing that you made the effort to do the best of which you are capable." To break down his point further, Coach included some explanations of how this philosophy of success applied to his overall approach to coaching:

1. "In my opinion, a mark received in class is no more valid a way to judge the success of a student than a score validly determines the success of a sporting event. It may determine a winner but not necessarily success."

2. "If you truly do your best, and only you really know, then you are successful and the actual score is immaterial whether it was favorable or unfavorable."

Coach Wooden said that although Arizona State had broken the press quickly and shot the ball extremely well, he liked the effect that the press had had on them. He thought Arizona State had just had a great day shooting and they would've been equally effective against whatever defense he had played. In spite of the score that came down against his own team, Coach was very pleased with the way the 2-2-1 press sped the game up. He decided that, in spite of the loss, he would keep the 2-2-1 press and bring it back the next year as the primary activator of his defense. March 20, 1965; New York City: The best high school player in the country, Lewis Alcindor (later known as Kareem Abdul Jabbar), watches the telecast of UCLA winning their second consecutive National Championship, defeating Michigan 91-80 using their now-famous 2-2-1 press to speed the game up. Alcindor decides UCLA might be the place he *wanted to play because he liked their pressing/fast break style. March 31, 1975; San Diego, California: UCLA defeats Kentucky 92-85 to give John Wooden his 10th National Championship in the last 12 seasons. Since that loss at Arizona State in 1963, Coach Wooden has now enjoyed a record of 44 wins and one loss in the NCAA Tournament. This includes seven straight National Championships and 38 consecutive wins in tournament games – and the 2-2-1 press had been a key ingredient. Sometimes when an individual, team, or business faces a loss, they want to change their strategy and try something new just because they aren't happy about the final numbers. Instead of looking at the big picture application of the lessons learned or the overall implications of the game, they are quick to embrace something different just because they are desperate to see a different result on the scoreboard. Those thinkers are sometimes referred to as* The Idea of the Month Club. *It's lucky for UCLA fans that John Wooden's definition of success prevented him from joining that club.*

John Wooden focused on the process, not the outcome. In fact, he never focused on winning. He focused on the culture, process, principles, people, and team building that produce wins. As a result, he won a lot. Yes, it took time but his principles and process paved the way for incredible sustained success.

Forget the Past, Focus on the Fundamentals

Jon Gordon

Past failure does not determine future failure. Past success does not determine future success. Future success is determined by

137

Beyond the 7 C's

what you do today. To build a winning team, you must help your players and staff have amnesia about past outcomes and remember all the little things they did to get better. In a wonderful article about Vince Lombardi and the Green Bay Packers, my friend James Clear wrote the following in his blog JamesClear.com:

It was July of 1961 and the 38 members of the Green Bay Packers football team were gathered together for the first day of training camp. The previous season had ended with a heartbreaking defeat when the Packers squandered a lead late in the 4th quarter and lost the NFL Championship to the Philadelphia Eagles. The Green Bay players had been thinking about this brutal loss for the entire off-season and now, finally, training camp had arrived and it was time to get to work. The players were eager to advance their game to the next level and start working on the details that would help them win a championship. Their coach, Vince Lombardi, had a different idea. In his best-selling book, When Pride Still Mattered: A Life Of Vince Lombardi, author David Maraniss explains what happened when Lombardi walked into training camp in the summer of 1961. He took nothing for granted. He began a tradition of starting from scratch, assuming that the players were blank slates who carried over no knowledge from the year before. . . . He began with the most elemental statement of all. "Gentlemen," he said, holding a pigskin in his right hand, "this is a football." Lombardi was coaching a group of three dozen professional athletes who, just months prior, had come within minutes of winning the biggest prize their sport could offer. And yet, he started from the very beginning.

Lombardi's methodical coverage of the fundamentals continued throughout training camp. Each player reviewed how to block and tackle. They opened up the playbook and started from page one. At some point, Max McGee, the Packers' Pro Bowl wide receiver, joked, "Uh, Coach, could you slow down a little. You're going too fast for us." Lombardi reportedly cracked a smile, but continued his obsession with the basics all the same. His team would become the best in the league at the tasks everyone else took for granted. Six months later, the Green Bay Packers beat the New York Giants 37-0 to win the Super Bowl. Vince Lombardi is carried off the field by his players after defeating the New York Giants 37-0 to win the 1961 NFL Championship. The 1961 season was the beginning of Vince Lombardi's reign as one of the greatest football coaches of all-time. He would never lose in the playoffs again. In total, Lombardi won five NFL Championships in a span of seven years, including three in a row. He never coached a team with a losing record.

The past is gone. Every year is a fresh start to focus on the process, develop your fundamentals, and build a winning team.

LOSS: Learning Opportunity, Stay Strong

Mike Smith

As a leader it's important to provide your team with the right perspective, especially after a loss. Every great team will experience losses on their journey. Only one team in the league can win the championship each year. I wrote this book after seven seasons with the Falcons. I won a lot my first five years. Some may say I lost the last two, but I don't consider it a loss. I've learned so much and know that whatever I decide to do going forward I will become wiser, stronger, and better and I help more people learn from my victories and defeats. I also shared the same mindset and belief with my teams. When we lost we analyzed why and identified ways we could improve. Every loss was a learning opportunity and we had to stay strong and positive in order to move forward. Your team's attitude and belief will determine how you deal with setbacks, challenges, and losses, so make sure from the beginning you spend as much time cultivating their belief system as you do your offensive system or defensive scheme. When adversity strikes, your belief system is the very thing that will get you through and help you triumph.

Culture Contamination

Jon Gordon

Leaders often ask me how long it takes to change a culture. My answer is, the more aligned everyone is, the less time it takes. If everyone buys into your vision, purpose, and belief system, culture change can happen very quickly. If you have energy vampires on your team, the process will take longer—and you probably won't be able to completely change your culture until they change or leave. The quicker you transform or remove the vampires from your team, the faster it takes to transform your culture. The longer you allow people from your old culture to contaminate your new culture, the longer it takes to change and build a team. If you want to build a winning team, you have to make sure everyone is all-in and you can't allow negative people from your old culture to impact the new mindset you are trying to build. The last thing you want is for negative veterans to contaminate positive rookies. This goes for sports, businesses, and schools. I've had the opportunity to work with Insight Global, the fastest growing technology staffing company in the United States, and discovered they won't hire people from outside the company. Their culture is the ultimate key to their success. It's so important that they don't want new employees who might bring negative energy to contaminate their culture. So they hire people who fit their culture right out of college and develop and promote from within. It's hard to argue with their track record and success.

Don't Focus on Winning Championships; Focus on Developing Champions

Jon Gordon

We hear it all the time. Coaches say, "We are going to win a championship." Players say their focus is to win a conference championship and then a national championship. It's all well and good but the truth is everyone in the country is writing down the same goals and saying the same things. Focusing on winning a championship doesn't mean you will win one. Instead, the focus should be on developing champions. To build a winning team, spend all your time and energy developing champions. Cultivate leadership, character, work ethic, grit, belief, and selflessness in each person on your team. Help

Beyond the 7 C's

them grow into great leaders and people. Teach them how champions think and act. When you do this, you'll find that champions do the right things and make plays that ultimately lead to championships. Of course there's no guarantee that you will win a championship even when you develop champions, but you'll give your team a greater chance and in the process create better human beings. This, I believe, is the purpose of sports. To create better human beings. When you develop champions you develop people who will change the world.

The Time Is Now

Mike Smith

There are three different time frames that we all live in. Each year I would share this concept with my team because to be successful, efficient, and healthy, everyone must make sure they spend the appropriate amount of time and energy in each time frame.

The first time frame is yesterday, the past. We have to learn from past experiences whether they resulted in positive or negative outcomes. When you use your past as an opportunity to grow in a positive way, it will pay dividends in the other two time frames. Many people spend way too much time reliving what happened yesterday and trying to justify what they are doing now because of it. The past has to be viewed as a springboard to the future. We have all been around people who spend too much time reminiscing about the past and what they have or have not accomplished. They spend so much time in the past that they don't focus on what they can do now to create their futures. The game is over. The mistake happened. You lost the business account. Find the lesson and move on. Don't be bitter. Get better.

The second time frame is tomorrow, the future. There is nothing wrong with looking forward to the future as long as you are using that time to improve and stay ahead of the curve. You just have to make sure you guard against fantasizing about a future that won't happen unless you take action to create it. You also want to make sure you don't spend your time worrying about the future that is not here yet. The angst that results can cause weak performance and morale problems on the team. Too many teams worry about the playoffs when they have half the season left. You can't worry about the future. You just have to take it one play, one game, at a time.

This brings us to the third time frame, which is today, the present. Some people call it living in the now. Jon calls it living in the moment and I don't know that there is any better way to describe it. When you are living in the moment you are immersing yourself in the process to be the absolute best that you can be right now. When you have a team that is focused on today and what they can do to make themselves better every moment, these series of moments will help you create a future that you love. Looking back on all the teams I have coached, the ones that were most successful were the ones that embraced the now and seized the moment. They had a vision for the future but they focused their energy in the present. They let go of their past mistakes and learned from them to make better decisions in the present, which lead to better results in the future. We need to utilize all three time frames, but we want to make sure we only live and focus on one—*today*.

Beyond the 7 C's

Looking for Murphy

Jon Gordon

Gus Bradley, the head coach of the Jacksonville Jaguars, told me about a great way he helps his team reframe a negative mindset and shift into a positive one. In sports a lot of negative things happen. Your team can be leading and all of a sudden your quarterback throws an interception and you lose the game. You might win a couple of games in a row and then you lose one of your key players. Unfortunately Murphy's Law comes into play. Anything that can go wrong will go wrong, and in sports it seems to always go wrong at the worst possible time. Instead of letting his players have a victim mindset when things go wrong, Gus reframes the situation. He doesn't say, "Just when everything was going great, this happened!" because he knows that would undermine morale. Instead Gus tells his team that they are looking for this guy Murphy who is a big jerk. They aren't waiting for Murphy to show up and ruin their day. Instead they are going to find him and when they do they are going to kick Murphy's butt. Instead of letting Murphy bring them down they focus on being mentally tougher to take on Murphy. So now the players expect to see Murphy but they have an even greater expectation that they will defeat him. Instead of a victim mindset they have a hero mindset. Victims and heroes both get knocked down but heroes get back up and, armed with belief and grit, turn the challenge into victory. To build a winning team, you'll need to help reframe situations and events from negative to positive. You will need to help your team take on the things that go wrong, and you'll all be stronger when you do.

144

Beyond the 7 C's

Pressure, Not Stress

Jon Gordon

Another lesson I learned from Gus is the difference between pressure and stress. Gus said that leaders put stress on their teams when they place expectations on them that are beyond the players' control. Focusing on outcomes such as goals, wins, points, and so on creates stress because you can't control how many wins you will have or how many points you will score. Saying "We had better win and we need to win" will only cause stress, which causes anxiety and weakens performance. As a coach you never ever want to put stress on your team. Instead, you want to apply pressure. Gus says that you should apply pressure on the things your team can control. Apply pressure when it comes to your team's effort, work ethic, knowledge of the playbook, preparation, process, and other things they can control, such as the fundamentals and teamwork. This is the approach John Wooden and Vince Lombardi took, and your team will perform better if you follow suit. As a leader you want to apply pressure, not stress.

Compete, then Unite

Mike Smith

The best teams, coaching staffs, and leadership groups that I have been associated with are the ones that were willing to challenge one another in meetings, game planning sessions, and practice. Everyone understood the challenge and that every action we took was predicated on making the team better. This means at times we would argue and fight in coaching meetings and game-planning sessions. One person would feel strongly about what would work, while another might disagree and have other suggestions. We understood that you couldn't take anything personally in these meetings. We had to be willing to disagree in order to consider all the possible plans and come up with the best one. It was uncomfortable at times because in our quest to get better there were always different views and strong opinions. These discussions, while difficult, were very healthy and ensured that we were utilizing the full talents and knowledge of our staff. Some of the best game plans that I have been involved in putting together were the ones that came out of the most disagreements and discussions, and some of the best wins came after meetings where not everyone agreed on our course of action. But here's the deal: Even though we may have disagreed, once the final decision was made, we united and every coach in that meeting adopted the plan and sold it to the players. You have to be unified when you are presenting plans to the players. When you leave the meeting room, your team's game plan for the week is set in stone. Everybody had an opportunity to contribute, so when we left the room we all took ownership of it. Another benefit of having this structure in meetings is that you eliminate the chance for there to be second guessing or Monday-morning quarterbacking from staff members. You compete in the meeting room and then you unite when you leave.

Competing on the field is just as important. Our goal every practice was to compete against each other to make each other better, but once it was game time, we united as one team to compete against our opponent. Competition followed by unity builds strong coaching staffs and teams.

Speaking as One Voice to the Media

Mike Smith

In Chapter 4, I talked about communicating your message to your team. Well, whether you are a head coach or the CEO of a large company, it is also very important to communicate and control your external messaging. With today's 24/7 news cycle and in our multi-channel, multi-blog, multi-platform environment, it is impossible to have only one person and one voice speak for the entire organization. The NFL, NCAA, NBA, and every other pro sports league all have rules in place that say you have to make players and coaches available to the media throughout the season and even at different times during the off-season, and other industries also require regular contact with the press. Even though you can't have just one voice speaking for your organization, you want to make sure all your voices are speaking as one.

Speaking as one voice starts with a communications department that has a complete understanding of the way information and news is gathered and disseminated. This is an ongoing evolution that has to be dealt with on a regular basis. Do not give it lip service. I would strongly suggest you have a media-training program in place to teach your team members how to handle the challenging questions they will be asked. It should also cover the pitfalls of irresponsible postings on Facebook, Twitter, Instagram, and other social media outlets. We have all seen the consequences of even one irresponsible tweet or negative comment about the team on social media. When it comes to the team and the workplace, people benefit from guidelines that encourage them to think before posting. Of course, players and other employees can voice their opinions, but they must be aware that when they make public remarks, they are representing the organization. An off-the-cuff comment can hurt the team, so social media education is crucial.

Speaking as one voice involves everyone on the team thinking about what they say before they say it. When someone speaks out, they should also be prepared to take responsibility for their comments. The last thing you want is information about your team attributed to an "unnamed source," "unnamed player," "unnamed coach," "unnamed member of the personnel department," or "a person close to the team on the condition of anonymity because he or she is not authorized to speak on the subject." Phrases like these are usually signs of an unhealthy environment in which individuals are putting their own interests in front of the team's. It's also a sign that as a leader you haven't addressed an issue up front, and it presents the team as fractured. You must be aware of these pitfalls and address them with your team before they become a problem. You don't want to wait until a crisis hits to start communicating with your team about these issues. It's too late then. You want to do it before so you can avoid a crisis. I recommend that you talk to your team about communicating as one voice that says things that build the team up instead of tearing it down. Complaints and issues should be addressed in the locker room and meeting rooms, not through the media. Nothing ever gets solved in the media and in most cases, it makes things worse. Dedicating resources to educate and assist members of the team or organization up front will limit the number of times that your PR department has to operate in damage-control mode. It will also reduce the chances of an inconsistent message coming from within the organization. Consistency in organizational messaging and media training will go a long way in minimizing issues both internally and externally. Many voices speaking as one help create a united team.

Become a Lifelong Learner

Mike Smith

We should all strive to be lifelong learners. Today it is easier than ever. Advancements in technology provide so many different platforms that present us with opportunities to learn from some of the greatest teachers and most successful people in the world. If you have an Internet connection or a couple of bars on your smartphone, you have access to a large reservoir of the world's learning materials. The opportunity is available to all of us and it is up to you to take advantage of it. Instead of relying on only your own experiences, take advantage of the opportunity to always advance yourself by learning from the experiences of others. But, as you seek out mentors in the digital world, do not forget the importance of finding mentors in the real world as well. One of the things I love most about the coaching world is that there are so many lifelong learners. It's common practice for coaches to call other coaches, visit with each other, and share ideas and best practices. In fact, it's more common at the professional and college levels than it is at the high-school level. I believe every coach at every level should seek out other leaders to learn from. It's a practice that would greatly benefit businesses and schools as well. Can you imagine how your business would grow if a sales manager met with a few sales managers from a different company or division and they exchanged best practices? Imagine what would happen if teachers from different schools could gather together and learn new techniques and syllabi.

I have had the opportunity to be around some of the most successful leaders in business and sports, and I try to learn as much as I can. When you get the chance to be around teachers, experts, and other people in your profession, act like a sponge and soak up all the wisdom you can. Take time to read about successful leaders and what they have to say about the art of leadership. Even if you have never had a chance to sit and talk with a great leader like coach John Wooden, you can learn from him by reading about his theories on coaching and leadership. Seek wisdom and you will be surprised how it forces you to use your brain-power in ways that you didn't think was possible. Challenge yourself and do not let a day go by in which you are not learning something new. The minute you think you know it all is the moment that you stop growing and improving.

Leave Your Legacy

Mike Smith

The coaches who I have had have influenced me more than anybody except my mother and father. I can tell you the name of every coach who I have ever had, in every sport that I have played, from little league and rec basketball, all the way through to the last coach I played for as a member of the Winnipeg Blue Bombers. From coach George Russell to coach Ray Jauch, I still remember fondly the different lessons I learned and experienced playing football, basketball, and baseball as a young kid. These coaches left an impression on me that has lasted a lifetime. I still vividly remember their styles of coaching and how they would find a way to bring a group of guys together to work toward a common goal. We did not always win but we learned many valuable lessons about teamwork, sportsmanship, leadership, and humility—and, most importantly, we learned that it is more about the journey and preparation for life than the game that we played.

If you are a coach, please never forget how much of an influence you are to the people you come in contact with. Even if you aren't a sports coach, every one of us can be a coach and influence the people around us. Everyone can leave a legacy by the way they lead and the impact they have on others. When you coach others and build a winning team you build winners for life. No statue, no building, or road named in your honor can compare to the legacy you leave in the lives of others.

The Action Plan

*Utilize the 7 C's to Build a Winning Team
and Organization*

1. Create your culture.

   - Build your culture up and down. Develop it in the boardroom and the locker room.

   - Since everyone creates your culture, make sure you engage and encourage all members of your organization to be involved.

   - Let everyone know your vision, purpose, and beliefs and make sure that your actions are in line with those beliefs and attitudes.

   - Identify what you and your team stand for. Once you know what you stand for, decisions are easy to make.

   - Remember that to build a great culture you have to build it, live it, value it, reinforce it, and fight for it.

2. Be positively contagious.

   - Decide to be a big dose of Vitamin C instead of a germ.

   - Create and share a powerful vision, mission, and purpose with your team. When possible, have your team create the vision, mission, and purpose together. This creates even more buy-in.

- Be contagious with optimism and positivity. Leadership is a transfer of belief and attitude.

- Strive to have as many positively contagious team members as possible. When you fill your team with positively contagious people you will see production, teamwork, and trust grow exponentially.

- Weed negativity from your team. Confront, transform, and remove the energy vampires and implement a No Complaining policy.

- Lead with passion so that all the members of the organization see and feel it.

3. Be consistent.

- Be the same leader whether you are winning or losing. Stick to your principles and philosophy through adversity and challenges.

- Be consistent with your actions as you strive to improve and grow.

- Address the disease of complacency with your team, let go of the past, and create a fresh start each year.

- Look for signs of complacency and don't allow your team to rest on their past success.

- Focus on continuous and consistent improvement.

- Stay humble and hungry.

4. Communicate.

- Communicate frequently with the team collectively and individually.

- Remember that where there is a void in communication, negativity will fill it.

- Listen to your team. Ask questions and truly listen. You will learn a lot and also develop great relationships and trust. It may also lead to new ideas and better ways of doing things.

- Take the temperature of your building and people daily. Walk around, ask questions, listen, and observe and you will gather critical information to help you lead your team in a positive direction.

- Reiterate and reinforce important messages to your team often. Say it so much that it almost becomes annoying to your team.

- Make sure every leader and person in your organization is sharing the same messages. Also make sure they are modeling the message.

- Utilize outside voices to reinforce messages and themes to your team.

- Be aware of the busyness and stress that can sabotage your communication and relationships.

- Create a communication structure so that your communication fosters collaboration.

5. Connect.
   - Understand that creating a connected team is one of the most important things you can do. Team beats talent when talent isn't a team.

   - Remember that X's and O's are overrated. Take time to slow down and connect with your team members. Culture and relationships are what win over time.

- Help your team to connect in meaningful ways instead of using technology. But use technology and texting to supplement communication and share encouragement.

- When team members connect and build strong relationships they don't just work with each other, they work for each other.

- Utilize team-building exercises where team members share meaningful stories and feelings. Hearts open, walls come crumbling down, and vulnerability turns into connection and strength.

- Connect on a personal level as well. Find ways to connect outside the building in order to be more connected inside the building and on the field.

- Stay connected. Don't assume your relationships are strong. You must continue to foster connections with your fellow leaders and team.

6. Commit.

- To be a great leader, coach, and team member you must be more than involved—you must be committed. Your team has to know that you are committed to them before they will commit to you.

- Your commitment must be greater than anyone else's in the organization.

- Lead in such a way that people feel your commitment.

- Demonstrate your commitment to your team through your actions.

- Make time for your team and use that time to make them better. When you focus on making your team better, you get better.

- Look for opportunities to serve your team and put the team first. You don't have to be great to serve but you have to serve to be great.

- Lose your ego and take ownership of problems instead of blaming others.

7. Care.

- Create a culture of caring. When you care for and about your team members they will perform at a much higher level.

- Value each team member as a person, not a number.

- Decide to be a transformational leader instead of a transactional leader. Love tough.

- Show your team you care about them. Take a personal interest in their specific roles in the organization and help them grow.

- Surround yourself with people who care.

- Build a team that cares about one another.

- Discover and share your own caring trademark.

The Big C

- Realize that today's leaders must also coach the people they lead.

- Focus on developing more leaders by coaching the people you lead.

- Ask the people you lead to share their vision and goals with you and then ask how you can help them achieve them.

The Other Big C

- Realize you can't build a winning team without character.

- Build a team with both character and talent.

- Continue to develop the character of your team.

Put the 7 C's to Work to Enhance Your Culture

Visit www.wininthelockerroom.com to:

- Print posters with memorable quotes from the book.
- Share *You Win in the Locker Room First*'s practical principles with your organization and team.
- Learn how other teams have utilized the 7 C's.

Build a Winning Team

I f you are interested in having Jon Gordon or Mike Smith speak to your organization or consult with your leadership team, contact The Jon Gordon Companies at:

Phone: (904) 285-6842

E-mail: info@jongordon.com

Online: JonGordon.com

Twitter: @jongordon11

Facebook: Facebook.com/JonGordonpage

Instagram: JonGordon11

Sign up for Jon Gordon's weekly e-newsletter at **JonGordon.com**.

To purchase bulk copies of *You Win in the Locker Room First* at a discount for large groups or your organization, please contact your favorite bookseller or Wiley's Special Sales group at specialsales@wiley.com or (800) 762-2974.

Other Books by Jon Gordon

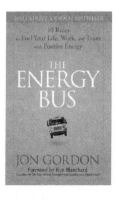

The Energy Bus

A man whose life and career are in shambles learns from a unique bus driver and set of passengers how to overcome adversity. Enjoy this enlightening ride of positive energy that is improving the way leaders lead, employees work, and teams function.

www.TheEnergyBus.com

The Energy Bus for Kids

This illustrated children's adaptation of the bestselling book *The Energy Bus* tells the story of George, who, with the help of his school bus driver Joy, learns that if he believes in himself, he'll find the strength to overcome any challenge. His journey teaches kids how to overcome negativity, bullies, and everyday challenges to be their best.

www.EnergyBusKids.com

The No Complaining Rule

Follow a VP of human resources who must save herself and her company from ruin, and discover proven principles and an actionable plan to win the battle against individual and organizational negativity.

www.NoComplainingRule.com

Training Camp

This inspirational story about a small guy with a big heart and a special coach who guides him on a quest for excellence reveals the eleven winning habits that separate the best individuals and teams from the rest.

www.TrainingCamp11.com

The Shark and the Goldfish

Delightfully illustrated, this quick read is packed with tips and strategies for responding to challenges beyond your control in order to thrive during waves of change.

www.SharkandGoldfish.com

Soup

The newly anointed CEO of a popular soup company is brought in to reinvigorate the brand and bring success back to a company that has fallen on hard times. Through her journey, discover the key ingredients to unite, engage, and inspire teams and create a culture of greatness.

www.Soup11.com

The Seed

Go on a quest for the meaning and passion behind work with Josh, an up-and-comer at his company who is disenchanted with his job. Through Josh's cross-country journey, you'll find surprising new sources of wisdom and inspiration in your own business and life.

www.Seed11.com

The Positive Dog

We all have two dogs inside of us. One dog is positive, happy, optimistic, and hopeful. The other dog is negative, mad, pessimistic, and fearful. These two dogs often fight inside us, but guess who wins the fight? The one you feed the most. *The Positive Dog* is an inspiring story that not only reveals the strategies and benefits of being positive but also highlights an essential truth for humans: Being positive doesn't just make you better. It makes everyone around you better.

www.feedthepositivedog.com

Other Books by Jon Gordon